INTERNATIONAL DEVELOPMENT IN FOCUS

# Greening National Development Financial Institutions

Trends, Lessons Learned, and Ways Forward

EMMA DALHUIJSEN, EVA GUTIERREZ, TATSIANA KLIATSKOVA,
RACHEL MOK, AND MARTIJN GERT JAN REGELINK

WORLD BANK GROUP

# Contents

## Boxes

## Figures

## Tables

# Foreword

Global pursuit of climate and environmental (C&E) objectives will require trillions of dollars of investment over the next decade. However, many countries, particularly low- and middle-income nations, are grappling with significant fiscal and economic constraints in the aftermath of pandemic-related disruptions to economic and social activity.

In this context, National Development Financial Institutions (NDFIs) are vital actors in mobilizing needed financing from private sources to meet countries' pressing needs. These financial institutions, typically state owned and driven by socioeconomic objectives, guide country development plans and policies. With their substantial assets—amounting to over US$19 trillion and accounting for more than 10 percent of global investments annually, NDFIs have the scale and influence to play a transformative role, especially in low- and middle-income countries, where public actors provide 60 percent of total climate financing, almost half by NDFIs.

NDFIs, when managed efficiently, can help overcome market barriers and mobilize private-sector financing for green investment, including through the provision of long-term financing, as well as innovative structuring of blended finance and credit enhancements. NDFIs can address existing market gaps by helping with structuring and co-financing long-term, high-risk projects and with surmounting obstacles such as extended payback periods and perceived project risk, particularly for projects in which social returns exceed financial returns. NDFIs have also helped create markets through transaction demonstration effects, having been the first issuers of green bonds in many countries. This unique position makes them effective in mobilizing finance from public and private investors for priority goals.

Like other financial institutions, NDFIs also face risks from climate change and environmental concerns in their investments and lending. Thus, they are aware of the importance of following emerging guidance on C&E risk management and disclosures from financial-sector supervisors and standard setters. NDFIs are also familiar with the application of environmental safeguards to limit negative impacts of their operations and can be an effective advocate for wider application of these good practices throughout emerging-market financial systems.

The World Bank Group stands ready to support NDFIs through funding and technical assistance to strengthen their governance and risk management while working closely with governments to create the preconditions for NDFIs to catalyze private funding for climate. This report is part of this effort. It offers a comprehensive analysis of the current trends and policy actions required to expand the "green" role of NDFIs. Drawing on a survey of 22 NDFIs from diverse regions and income levels, as well as in-depth case studies of selected institutions, the report presents recommendations to enhance the efficiency, effectiveness, and environmental impact of their investments. It also emphasizes the importance of pipeline preparation and private capital mobilization to boost green financing.

We look forward to working with these financial institutions to apply the lessons from this report, expand C&E investments, and move closer to the scale of public and private funding required to reverse climate change.

**Jean Pesme**
*Global Director of Finance*
*Finance, Competitiveness, and Innovation Global Practice*
*World Bank*

# Acknowledgments

This publication is a product of the World Bank's Finance, Competitiveness, and Innovation Global Practice with financial support from the Global Program on Sustainability and the Climate Support Facility. This work was prepared by Emma Dalhuijsen, senior financial sector specialist; Eva Gutierrez, lead financial economist; Tatsiana Kliatskova, financial sector economist; Rachel Mok, financial sector specialist; and Martijn Gert Jan Regelink, senior financial sector specialist, all of the World Bank. Pablo Saavedra, vice president, Equitable Growth, Finance, and Institutions; Jean Pesme, global director of finance; and Loic Chiquier, senior adviser, provided overall guidance. The team thanks Christina Ann Davis for editorial support and Datapage for design and layout assistance.

The team would like to thank senior officials of the National Development Financial Institutions who participated in the survey. We are also very grateful to senior officials of the Fideicomisos Instituidos en Relación con la Agricultura (FIRA, in Mexico), the Korea Development Bank (in the Republic of Korea), Türkiye Sinai Kalkinma Bankasi (in Türkiye), and the Development Bank of Southern Africa (in South Africa) who shared their data and insights with us for in-depth case studies.

We are grateful for the substantive feedback received from the peer reviewers—Louise Gardiner, Africa coordinator, Sustainable Banking and Finance Network, International Finance Corporation; Thomas Michael Kerr, lead climate change specialist, World Bank; Rodrigo Pereira Porto, financial sector consultant, World Bank; and Angel Manuel O'Dogherty Madrazo, general director of sectoral intelligence, FIRA. The team also benefited from review and insights from country teams and the World Bank Country Management Units covering the countries mentioned in this publication. Any errors or omissions in the data or interpretations are attributable solely to the authors of the work.

CSF
CLIMATE SUPPORT FACILITY

# About the Authors

**Emma Dalhuijsen** is a senior financial sector specialist at the World Bank, advising governments and central banks on the development of green financing markets and the integration of climate and environmental (C&E) financial risks into supervisory frameworks and financial regulation. Prior to the World Bank, she worked at the Bank of England, coordinating its supervisory response to climate risk, and at the Dutch Central Bank. She also is a board member of ElleSolaire, a social enterprise supporting women's empowerment through clean energy entrepreneurship. Emma has an MSc in economic history from the London School of Economics and a BSc in economics and BA in history from the University of Amsterdam.

**Eva Gutierrez** is a lead financial economist in the Latin America and the Caribbean Region of the World Bank. She has worked on state-owned bank reform in more than 20 countries through advisory and lending operations, including Brazil, Colombia, Ecuador, Mexico, Turkmenistan, Uzbekistan, and Viet Nam. She developed the guidance note to assess performance of State-Owned Financial Institutions, part of the World Bank Integrated State-Owned Framework, and the guidance note to evaluate the role of the state in the provision of financial services in the context of the Financial Sector Assessment Program, implemented by the International Monetary Fund (IMF) and the World Bank. She has led the World Bank Community of Practice for State-Owned Enterprises. She is leading projects supporting the development of a sustainable finance taxonomy and formulation for environmental, social, and governance guidelines for commercial banks in Mexico. She has published articles on various financial topics, including development bank reform and the resolution of state-owned banks and cooperative banks. Prior to joining the World Bank, she worked at the IMF, with a focus on macrofinancial issues. Eva has a PhD in economics from Boston University, a master's degree in financial economics from the Center for Monetary and Financial Studies, Madrid, and a bachelor's degree in economics from the Universidad de Murcia in Murcia, Spain.

**Tatsiana Kliatskova** is a financial sector economist in the South Asia Finance, Competitiveness, and Innovation Global Practice of the World Bank. Prior to joining the World Bank, she was a research fellow at the Deutsche Bundesbank and a research associate at DIW Berlin. Her main research and policy interests include the role of the state in development and finance, bank regulation and supervision, and capital markets development. Tatsiana has a PhD in economics from the Free University of Berlin, Germany, and a master's degree in economic policy from the Central European University in Budapest, Hungary.

**Rachel Mok** is a financial sector specialist for the Southern and Eastern Africa Unit of the World Bank, where she primarily develops technical assistance programs, operations, and policy diagnostics related to greening countries' financial systems. Examples of her work include developing approaches to deepen green financing (for example, in the context of greening National Development Banks, developing green financing instruments such as labeled bonds or loans, and stimulating the private and financial sector's engagement in carbon markets) and working with central banks and financial regulators to enhance the assessment and management of climate-related financial risks. In addition, she has supported the development of the World Bank's corporate strategy on climate finance, which aims to identify ways in which the International Finance Corporation, the Multilateral Investment Guarantee Agency, and the World Bank could work together to scale up climate finance for client countries. She also works on programs related to carbon pricing and carbon markets, including through the Partnership for Market Implementation, Networked for Carbon Markets initiative, and Invest for Climate programs. Rachel has an MSc in environmental technology from Imperial College London and a BSc in geography with economics from the London School of Economics and Political Science, United Kingdom.

**Martijn Gert Jan Regelink** is a senior financial sector specialist in the Finance, Competitiveness, and Innovation Global Practice of the World Bank. He leads the World Bank's advisory services on C&E risks for the financial sector, providing policy advice to regulators and supervisors around the world. In addition, he represents the World Bank in the Network for Greening the Financial System and Financial Stability Board working groups on climate risk. Previous experience includes working as a strategy adviser to the board of the Dutch Central Bank, where he spearheaded the bank's inaugural program focusing on climate risks. Martijn has an MSc in international economics and business and an MA in international relations and organizations, both from Groningen University, the Netherlands.

# Executive Summary

National Development Financial Institutions (NDFIs) are crucial for mobilizing the required financing, including from private sources, to reach countries' climate and environmental (C&E) objectives. Funding needed to achieve countries' C&E goals is in the trillions of dollars. At the same time, many countries are also facing significant fiscal and economic constraints. Low-income and middle-income countries (LICs and MICs), other than China, need an estimated US$783 billion per year in additional investments for climate action through 2030 (World Bank 2023). NDFIs have the scale to play an essential role in mobilizing the required financing from public and private sources toward C&E goals.

NDFIs are well positioned to overcome market barriers associated with green investments and catalyze private-sector financing. NDFIs, when adequately managed, can address market failures and create new markets. Compared to private investors, NDFIs have a stronger appetite for financing long-term, high-risk investments and can thus overcome market barriers associated with green investments, such as long payback periods and high perceived project risk. NDFIs have the tools to support private capital mobilization through de-risking instruments and blended financing. Moreover, NDFIs can enable private capital mobilization by supporting the generation of a green project pipeline and through demonstration transactions that stimulate market creation. Given the limited capacity of governments to scale up C&E financing owing to current fiscal conditions, NDFIs' role in mobilizing private financing will be critical to closing the C&E financing gaps.

At the same time, NDFIs must manage the risks that climate and other environmental concerns present to their investment and lending operations. NDFIs, like other financial institutions (FIs), are exposed to the impacts of physical risks—financial risks stemming from the effects of climate change, environmental degradation, and loss of nature on the economy—as well as transition risks originating from the realignment of economies with C&E goals. In addition, lack of compliance with good C&E practices and regulations can affect the financial performance of assets or result in reputational risks for the institution. Moving forward, NDFIs should respond to emerging guidance set by financial-sector supervisors and standard setters to better manage and disclose C&E risks at the institutional, project, and portfolio levels.

The main purpose of this publication is to take stock of the current trends and recommend policy actions for "greening" NDFIs. The report identifies key steps NDFIs can take to catalyze finance toward countries' C&E objectives and manage C&E risks. The assessment of NDFIs' C&E practices is based on a review of key elements of NDFI operations and their institutional setup. It draws from the results of a survey conducted by the World Bank of greening practices within NDFIs based in countries in a range of regions and income levels,[1] as well as on in-depth case studies of four NDFIs:

1. Fideicomisos Instituidos en Relación con la Agricultura (FIRA, in Mexico),

2. Korea Development Bank (KDB, in the Republic of Korea),

3. Türkiye Sinai Kalkinma Bankasi (TSKB, in Türkiye), and

4. Development Bank of Southern Africa (DBSA, in South Africa).

Results of a survey of NDFIs (refer to figure ES.1) conducted by the World Bank show that the majority of NDFIs have adopted green goals in their strategy and governance and that a few have set specific targets linked to Paris Agreement or other climate commitments. More than 80 percent of the survey respondents have set green objectives and prepared strategies to green their portfolios, often accommodated within the existing development mission and strategy of the institution. About two-thirds of respondents have made public pledges or commitments to align with international or national climate goals. However, only a few institutions have set specific targets or disclosed their contributions to C&E targets such as the Paris Agreement's Nationally Determined Contributions (NDCs). The majority of surveyed NDFIs have set green financing targets and excluded financing of some nongreen projects. Over half of the surveyed NDFIs have incorporated environmental and social considerations into their governance arrangements, often supported by specific policies and strategies, and many have created dedicated units or high-level committees to address C&E topics.

NDFIs are leading players in public climate finance, but the share of green assets in their portfolio remains low, with limited adaptation financing and

**FIGURE ES.1**

**Key results of NDFI survey**

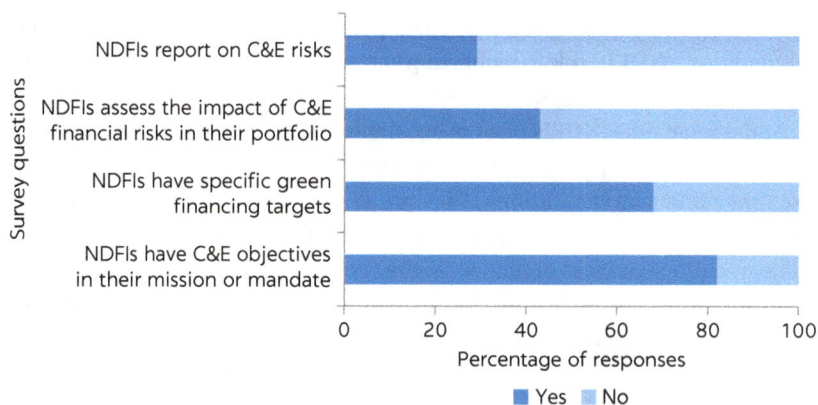

Source: Figure original to this publication and based on self-reporting by 22 NDFIs.
Note: C&E = climate and environmental; NDFI = National Development Financial Institution.

private capital mobilization. NDFIs provide around 22 percent of total global climate financing and the majority of public climate finance, especially in LICs and MICs.[2] However, although NDFIs are critical players in public climate financing, the share of green assets in their credit portfolios is still relatively low, with most survey respondents reporting green assets of less than 20 percent of credit portfolios, or 14 percent on average. For the few surveyed institutions that monitor climate adaptation and mitigation finance, climate finance is strongly biased toward mitigation, mainly through direct lending, with limited exposure to climate adaptation. Only a handful of the surveyed NDFIs target and track the mobilization of private capital, including through co-financing with other FIs. Surveyed NDFIs use green and sustainability-linked debt instruments to fund their green ambitions. However, use of these instruments remains limited. Perceived challenges by NDFIs to scaling up green financing include an unsupportive policy environment, a funding gap, and lack of knowledge and awareness of C&E issues on both the clients' and NDFIs' sides.

Moreover, C&E risk management and disclosure practices are still nascent. So far, surveyed NDFIs have been introducing C&E risks mainly through the lens of environmental and social risk management systems. Institutions assess these risks at the loan origination level with a focus on the impacts of loans and investments on C&E factors, instead of the financial risks. Although these systems are still basic in many cases, the majority of the surveyed NDFIs have developed some definition or classification system for green projects. At the same time, most NDFIs are not assessing and managing exposures to C&E financial risks at the portfolio and balance sheet levels or integrating this information into strategy and governance arrangements. Lack of data, standardized methodologies, and technical capacity are cited as critical challenges to mainstream C&E risk management practices. Moreover, while some of the surveyed NDFIs have public sustainability reports, C&E financial disclosures in line with international guidance are mainly absent.

NDFIs can take various actions to boost green financing, including through private capital mobilization, and to improve the management and disclosure of C&E risks (refer to figure ES.2).

- **NDFIs should introduce internal governance and strategy arrangements to support the prioritization of green objectives and ensure stakeholder coordination.** Governance arrangements should include strong board involvement and coordination mechanisms. A strategy should cover the complete set of activities across green financing and C&E risk dimensions. It should also communicate clear targets, including the targeted share of green assets. The strategies could consider broader contextual priorities set out by the NDCs and align with global agendas around the Paris Agreement. NDFIs should also build the required expertise across the organization by leveraging international and national networks.
- **To increase green financing, pipeline preparation and private capital mobilization should take center stage.** NDFIs can support the enabling environment for private capital through the development of bankable projects using technical assistance, market education, standardization of application procedures, and the creation of project preparation facilities. Improved access to international concessional climate funds can further support NDFIs to finance their ambitions. Where possible, NDFIs should explore using more

innovative instruments (beyond direct lending activities) to catalyze private finance. This includes increasing focus on blended and equity financing, as well as scaling up the use and piloting of innovative green instruments, such as sustainability-linked bonds and loans to incentivize green performance. NDFIs should also expand their offerings in critical development areas that generate important global or domestic public goods, such as adaptation and nature-based financing.

- **A better and more systemic understanding of C&E financial risks is an important first step to informing C&E risk management practices.** NDFIs should adopt comprehensive C&E risk management approaches that consider C&E risks from both the impact and the financial risk angles—that is,

**FIGURE ES.2**

**Overview of key recommendations for NDFIs, authorities, and development partners**

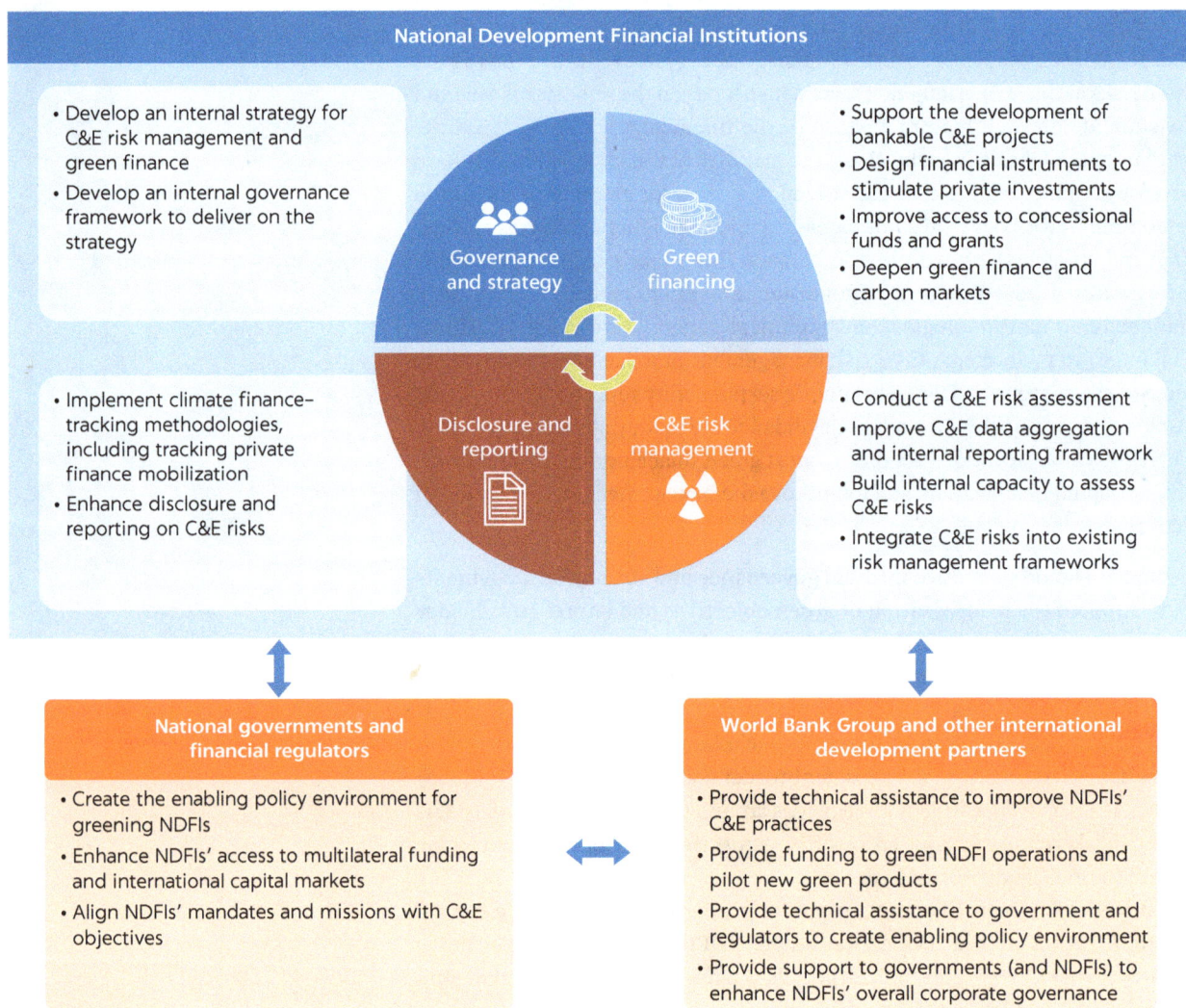

*Source:* Figure original to this publication.
*Note:* C&E = climate and environmental; NDFI = National Development Financial Institution.

covering potential risks generated by the institutions, as well as financial risks to their balance sheets. NDFIs could conduct exposure and forward-looking assessments, including more advanced tools such as scenario analysis and stress testing, to better understand the impact and materiality of C&E financial risks on NDFIs' credit and investment portfolios. These efforts should be supported by harmonizing and obtaining relevant data. Based on initial findings of the risk assessment, NDFIs could integrate C&E risks into their risk management process, internal control frameworks, and capital and liquidity adequacy assessment processes.

- **NDFIs should enhance their C&E disclosure and reporting practices,** which is an important means to facilitate communication with clients, beneficiaries, and other stakeholders. Disclosures should build on Task Force on Climate-Related Financial Disclosures (TCFD) guidance and International Sustainability Standards Board (ISSB) guidance. Equally, NDFIs should aim to improve the quality, transparency, and consistency of green financing tracking methodologies, including methodologies that track the amount of private finance mobilized.

Governments, financial-sector regulators, and Multilateral Development Banks (MDBs), including the World Bank, have an essential role in supporting the greening of NDFIs. Governments and other financial-sector authorities have a crucial role in shaping the enabling environment for greening NDFIs. This involves several key actions, such as developing ambitious national C&E targets, integrating NDFIs into the implementation of NDCs, establishing supportive legislation and policies (for example, carbon pricing and sector regulations), as well as developing financial-sector policies and regulations (for example, a green taxonomy or prudential regulations). Governments can incentivize further integration of C&E considerations into NDFIs' mandates, strategies, business models, and investment targets. The World Bank and other MDBs could provide targeted support through

- Technical assistance for NDFIs to build their capacity on C&E risk management and green financing,
- Funding to NDFIs that are looking to green their operations, and
- Support to authorities to create the enabling environment for greening NDFIs.

As NDFIs scale up operations to meet green financing needs, it is essential to enhance NDFIs' efficiency and effectiveness by ensuring that they are effectively managed and properly supervised. To improve efficiency, governments could incentivize the greening of state-owned NDFIs by integrating C&E and private capital mobilization considerations into NDFIs' mandates or missions and aligning incentives throughout the institution by using effective shareholder functions. NDFIs should maintain financial sustainability, beyond subsidies, limiting the scope of subsidized lending with a view to avoiding crowding out the private sector, fostering innovation, and reducing incentives for corruption. Financial supervisory authorities should ensure that NDFIs are properly supervised and operate on a level playing field related to prudential regulations and competition. In cases where the environment is not supportive of NDFI effectiveness, it may be advisable to operate in a second tier through other financial intermediaries.

## NOTES

1. The results of the survey cover responses from 22 NDFIs accounting for about 9 percent of global NDFI assets. Although the results of the survey are not necessarily representative for the whole universe of NDFIs, they are used to showcase the best practices of NDFIs in developing and pursuing a green agenda.
2. According to the Climate Policy Initiative, the average climate finance provided by NDFIs in 2019–2020 was US$145 billion, or 22 percent of total climate financing, representing the majority of public climate financing in that period (CPI 2022).

## BIBLIOGRAPHY

CPI (Climate Policy Initiative). 2022. *Global Landscape of Climate Finance: A Decade of Data.* https://www.climatepolicyinitiative.org/wp-content/uploads/2022/10/Global-Landscape -of-Climate-Finance-A-Decade-of-Data.pdf

World Bank. 2022. *What You Need to Know about Net Zero.* Washington, DC: World Bank. https://www.worldbank.org/en/news/feature/2022/05/23/what-you-need-to-know -about-net-zero#:~:text=Technically%2C%20global%20net%20zero%20will,be%20 released%20into%20the%20atmosphere.

World Bank. 2023. *Spending Needs to Address Selected Global Challenge.* Background note for the Evolution Roadmap. Unpublished.

# Glossary

**Climate adaptation and resilience** is a response to global warming that seeks to reduce the vulnerability of social and biological systems to the impact of climate change.

**Climate finance** is all lending and investments drawn from public, private, and alternative sources to support mitigation and adaptation actions that will address climate change.

**Climate mitigation** consists of actions to limit the magnitude or rate of long-term global warming and its related effects.

**Climate physical risks** are (financial) risks resulting from the physical impacts of climate change. This could include acute hazards (that is, event-driven hazards, including more frequent and intense extreme events such as cyclones or heat waves) and chronic hazards (that is, long-term changes in climate patterns, such as temperature rise).

**Climate risk** is a broad term capturing climate physical and transition risks.

**Climate scenario analysis** explores potential climate risk outcomes. By examining a wide range of scenarios, this approach can help explain uncertainties and estimate tail risks.

**Climate stress testing** is applying scenario analysis to evaluate the resiliency of the financial sector or individual institutions to shocks caused by the effects of severe but plausible climate scenarios. Stress tests for climate risks are typically explorative in nature and have so far not been used as pass/fail exercises or to increase capital requirements for financial institutions (FIs).

**Climate transition risks** are (financial) risks that can result from the process of adjustment toward a lower-carbon and more circular economy, prompted, for example, by changes in climate and environmental policy, technology, market, and consumer sentiment.

**Environmental risks** cover climate physical risks, transition risks, and non-climate change–related environmental risks such as local air pollution and loss of biodiversity.

**Financial institutions (FIs)** are financial-sector firms, including banks, pension funds, insurance companies, asset managers, brokerage firms, and investment dealers.

**Green financing** includes all lending and investments that contribute to climate mitigation, adaptation, and resilience and to other environmental objectives, including biodiversity management.

**Greening the financial system** is the role of all actors in the financial sector in mobilizing investments and lending toward green goals and managing climate-related and environmental risks.

**Greenwashing** is the practice of marketing financial products as green when in fact they do not meet climate-related or environmental standards.

**National Development Financial Institutions (NDFIs)** are any type of financial institution that a national government fully or partially owns or controls and that has been given an explicit legal mandate to reach socioeconomic goals in a region, sector, or market segment. Development Banks are the largest NDFIs, but other institutions, such as public credit guarantee funds, public trust funds, or public credit agencies, are included under the NDFI definition.

**Nationally Determined Contributions (NDCs)** are a central element for implementing the Paris Agreement and represent a country government's plan for national climate actions, including climate-related targets, policies, and measures.

**Net-zero greenhouse gas (GHG) emissions** will be achieved globally when human-caused GHG emissions have been reduced to the absolute minimum levels feasible and any remaining "residual emissions" are balanced by an equivalent quantity of permanent anthropogenic removals so that they cannot be released into the atmosphere. The term *anthropogenic removal* refers to the withdrawal of GHGs from the atmosphere through deliberate human activities, for instance, by technological solutions (direct air capture and storage) or by natural solutions (land restoration and improved forest management).

**Paris Agreement** is a legally binding international treaty on climate change that was adopted by 196 Parties at COP (Conference of the Parties) 21 in Paris on December 12, 2015, and entered into force on November 4, 2016.

**Public authorities** cover government ministries or government agencies, as well as supervisors and central banks. This report targets financial policymakers (for example, ministries of finance, central banks, and financial regulators and supervisors).

**Sustainable finance** includes all lending and investment that contributes to environmental, social, and governance (ESG) or other sustainable development–related goals.

# Abbreviations

| | |
|---|---|
| AFD | Agence Française de Développement |
| BCBS | Basel Committee on Banking Supervision |
| BNDES | Brazilian Development Bank |
| C&E | climate and environmental |
| CFF | Climate Finance Facility |
| CPI | Climate Policy Initiative |
| DB | Development Bank |
| DBSA | Development Bank of Southern Africa (South Africa) |
| DFI | Development Financial Institution |
| E&S | environmental and social |
| EIB | European Investment Bank |
| ERET | TSKB Environmental and Social Risk Evaluation Tool |
| ESG | environmental, social, and governance |
| ESRM | environmental and social risk management |
| ESS | environmental and social standards |
| FI | financial institution |
| FIRA | Fideicomisos Instituidos en Relación con la Agricultura (Mexico) |
| GCF | Global Climate Fund |
| GDP | gross domestic product |
| GEF | Global Environmental Facility |
| GHG | greenhouse gas |
| HIC | high-income country |
| IADB | Inter-American Development Bank |
| IC | investment concept |
| IDFC | International Development Finance Club |
| IFC | International Finance Corporation |
| IFO | International Financial Organization |
| ISDA | Integrated Sustainable Development Approach |
| ISSB | International Sustainability Standards Board |
| KDB | Korea Development Bank (the Republic of Korea) |
| KFW | Kreditanstalt für Wiederaufbau (Germany) |
| LIC | low-income country |

| | |
|---|---|
| LMIC | lower-middle-income country |
| MDB | Multilateral Development Bank |
| MIC | middle-income country |
| MSME | micro, small, and medium enterprise |
| NDB | National Development Bank |
| NDC | Nationally Determined Contribution (per Paris Agreement) |
| NDFI | National Development Financial Institution |
| SARAS | Sistema de Administracion de Riesgos Ambientales y Sociales (FIRA) |
| SDG | Sustainable Development Goal (per United Nations) |
| SOE | State-Owned Enterprise |
| SOFI | State-Owned Financial Institution |
| TCFD | Task Force on Climate-Related Financial Disclosures |
| TNFD | Taskforce on Nature-Related Financial Disclosures |
| TSKB | Türkiye Sinai Kalkinma Bankasi |
| UMIC | upper-middle-income country |
| UN | United Nations |
| UNDP | United Nations Development Programme |
| UNEP | United Nations Environment Programme |

| | |
|---|---|
| € | euro |
| US$ | US dollars |
| ₩ | won |

# 1 Introduction

## BACKGROUND

Funding needed to reach countries' climate and environmental (C&E) objectives is in the trillions of dollars at a time when many countries face significant fiscal and economic constraints. Low-income and middle-income countries (LICs and MICs), other than China, need an estimated US$783 billion per year in additional investments for climate action—to recover education and investment losses from the pandemic and to address conflict and fragility—through 2030 (World Bank 2023). Investment needs could increase sharply if interventions are delayed, spending is inefficient, or policies are inadequate (Rozenberg and Fay 2019).

Green financing can improve long-term fiscal sustainability and resilience, as well as enhance countries' competitiveness and growth; however, the large funding needs for C&E action come at a time when many countries are facing broader development challenges. Slowing growth, rising food and energy prices, high levels of public and private debt, and growing fiscal constraints are exacerbated by rising interest rates globally, the persistence of the COVID-19 pandemic, and the impact of the war in Ukraine (World Bank 2022b). Under such circumstances, LICs and MICs face difficult trade-offs between competing investment needs and are struggling to mobilize public and private resources required for their climate, environmental, and development priorities.

Recognition is growing that C&E physical and transition risks could negatively affect countries' economies and financial sectors. Physical risks stem from the short- and long-term effects of climate change, environmental degradation, and natural disasters such as sea level rise, droughts, floods, and hurricanes. Transition risks originate from efforts to mitigate climate change and improve environmental conditions by greening the economy, which may create economic adjustment costs in a broad range of sectors. One estimate suggests that insufficient action on climate change could cost the global economy US$178 trillion by 2070, almost double the current global gross domestic product (GDP) (Deloitte 2022; World Bank 2022c). At the same time, climate change and other factors are leading to irreversible, nonlinear impacts on biodiversity and ecosystem services. Estimates suggest that this issue could lead to a reduction in GDP of more than 10 percent in LICs and MICs in 2030

(Johnson et al. 2021). These impacts could, in turn, adversely impact the financial sector if they are not anticipated by financial institutions (FIs).

To respond to these risks, an increasing number of central banks and supervisors have begun to reform their supervisory framework to encourage FIs to better assess, disclose, and manage C&E risks. Standard-setting bodies are also starting to introduce guidance and principles to promote a common understanding around how climate-related financial risks can be effectively managed.[1]

This report aims to take stock of the current trends and recommends policy actions for "greening" National Development Financial Institutions (NDFIs).[2] By examining the current state and trends across different dimensions, as discussed later, this publication aims to identify steps that NDFIs could take to catalyze finance toward countries' C&E objectives and to manage C&E risks. It also identifies priority actions that country governments, Multilateral Development Banks (MDBs) (including the World Bank), and financial regulators could take to create an enabling environment for greening NDFIs.

## NATIONAL DEVELOPMENT FINANCIAL INSTITUTIONS

NDFIs are well positioned to play an essential role in mobilizing the required financing toward countries' C&E objectives. The collective scale of NDFI assets (close to US$19 trillion) significantly exceeds that of the multilateral system, and NDFI financing activities represent over 10 percent of global investments annually.[3]

In this context, NDFIs could play an important role in addressing C&E challenges. First, the involvement of NDFIs in the provision of green financing can be justified by their role in addressing market failures, including those arising from externalities that result in underfunding of projects with large social returns, such as green projects (Levy-Yeyati, Micco, and Panizza 2004). Thus, NDFIs often fulfill development objectives by financing projects that the private sector is unwilling or unable to finance—for example, in such underserved sectors as agriculture and micro, small, and medium enterprises (de la Torre, Gozzi, and Schmukler 2007; Gutierrez et al. 2011; Hainz and Hakenes 2012; World Bank 2012). Furthermore, as compared to private investors, NDFIs usually have a stronger appetite for financing long-term, high-risk investments and can thus address critical market barriers associated with green investments, such as long payback periods and high perceived project risks.

Second, NDFIs can have considerable influence on a country's development and investment plans and policies owing to their proximity to policymakers, local markets, and international development finance. Third, NDFIs can crowd in private investment for green activities by developing innovative approaches such as blended financing, co-financing, and de-risking instruments. Finally, NDFIs can also play a role in creating private capital to enable environmental projects by building a track record on green investments and acting as a first mover in financing demonstration projects at the early stages of market development. NDFIs can also provide technical assistance and capacity building at all stages of project development.

As with any other FIs, NDFIs must properly identify and manage the risks that C&E factors pose to their portfolios. As such, NDFIs should consider C&E risks beyond the lens of environmental and social risk management (ESRM) systems—that is, assessing environmental and social risks at the loan origination level with a focus on the impacts of loans and investments on C&E factors—and also consider the financial risks C&E factors pose to their balance sheets. C&E risks include physical risks—that is, financial risks stemming from the effects of climate change, environmental degradation, and loss of nature on the economy— as well as transition risks originating from the realignment of economies with C&E goals. In addition, lack of compliance with good C&E practices and regulations can affect the financial performance of assets or result in reputational risks for the institution.

There is wide recognition of the role of NDFIs in the attainment of green objectives, despite concerns over state ownership of these entities. Main concerns include, for example, crowding out private investments, inefficient management of resources, creating competition with commercial banks, and supporting the objectives of political elites, rather than addressing sustainable development objectives. Despite these concerns, 74 new NDFIs were established during the period 2010–20. The European Commission and the United Nations have expressed strong support for NDFIs (Gutierrez and Kliatskova 2021), with the G20 (Group of Twenty) and the World Bank similarly recognizing the important role of public development banks toward the achievement of the United Nations Sustainable Development Goals (SDGs) and the Paris Agreement (World Bank 2022a).

The conceptual framework for the assessment of NDFIs' C&E practices is based on the review of key elements of NDFI operations and their institutional setup. The framework is based on the World Bank State-Owned Financial Institution (SOFI) diagnostics,[4] which includes three pillars: functional, economic, and operational. The functional pillar assesses the mandate or mission of the institution, its operations, and its alignment between operations and mandate. The economic and financial assessment pillar examines the economic and financial performance of the SOFI. Finally, the operational assessment pillar evaluates the adequacy of the legal and oversight framework, corporate governance, risk management practices, and monitoring and evaluation practices.

For the evaluation of NDFI C&E practices, this report focuses on the functional assessment aspects (mandate or mission and operations) and the operational aspects, excluding the legal and regulatory framework under which the institutions operate.[5] The key elements of the assessment include the following modules (refer to figure 1.1):

FIGURE 1.1

**Modules of assessment of NDFI C&E practices**

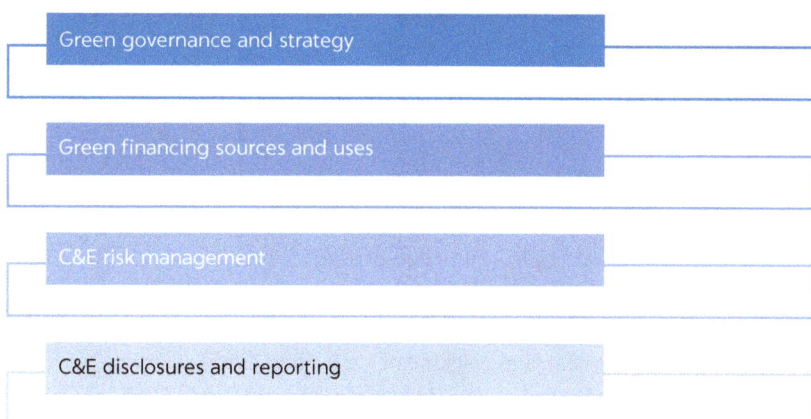

Green governance and strategy

Green financing sources and uses

C&E risk management

C&E disclosures and reporting

*Source:* Figure original to this publication.
*Note:* C&E = climate and environmental; NDFI = National Development Financial Institution.

- **Green governance and strategy:** Addressing C&E risks and opportunities requires the boards and senior management of NDFIs to be committed and engaged. This module assesses NDFIs' strategies, internal organization and governance structures, and allocation of adequate resources to effectively integrate C&E considerations into NDFIs' operations.
- **Green financing sources and uses:** This module focuses on NDFIs' support of investments critical for achieving a country's C&E objectives. In addition, it assesses NDFIs' role in catalyzing private finance toward C&E actions through blended financing or co-financing, credit enhancements, and de-risking instruments (for example, guarantees). Finally, the module examines NDFIs' ability to leverage different mechanisms to ensure that they have sufficient funding to support green investments, including accessing national and international climate funds and engaging in green financing markets (for example, by issuing green bonds).
- **C&E risk management:** NDFIs can use various techniques to identify, assess, and manage C&E risks. Beyond approaches used in ESRM systems, tools for identifying and assessing C&E financial risks include surveys, interviews, exposure analysis, scenario analysis, and stress testing.
- **C&E disclosures and reporting:** This module examines NDFIs' application of green definitions and taxonomy frameworks to determine what activities contribute to C&E objectives and enhancement of C&E disclosure and reporting in line with international standards. These approaches are used by NDFIs to enhance market transparency and understanding of C&E risks and opportunities.

The role of NDFIs in the green and broader sustainability agenda is getting increasing attention, with several guidance notes and reports on the topic having recently been developed. For example, the United Nations Development Programme (UNDP) has published a paper on the role of public development banks in scaling up sustainable finance (UNDP 2022).[6] The International Development Finance Club (IDFC), with support from the Institute for Climate Economics (I4CE) and the New Climate Institute, has developed an operationalizing framework, which includes a set of principles and tools for aligning NDFIs' financial flows with the Paris Agreement (Lütkehermöller et al. 2021). In addition, the Inter-American Development Bank has developed a guidebook for National Development Banks (NDBs) on climate risk, which provides a roadmap for integrating climate risks into NDBs' lending strategies and portfolio management (IADB 2021).

## ANALYSIS FOR THIS PUBLICATION

The analysis for this publication builds on existing analytical work, a qualitative survey, and interviews with a selection of NDFIs. It builds on the wealth of research that has already been conducted to identify priority actions for greening NDFIs as well as on a survey conducted by the World Bank in January 2022. The survey includes questions on (a) NDFIs' high-level commitments to the green agenda; (b) provision and tracking of green financing; (c) sources of funding, including access to green funding; (d) management of C&E risks; and (e) challenges and aspirations for greening the NDFIs (further details on the survey methodology is provided in appendix A). The responses were received from 22 NDFIs, with wide geographical and income-level coverage. The distribution of the 22 NDFIs by income level is as follows: 3 are from high-income, 13 are from upper-middle-income, 4 are from lower-middle-income, and 2 are from low-income countries. By region of operation, 8 NDFIs are based in Latin America, 4 are in Europe and Central Asia, 5 are in East Asia and the Pacific, 3 are in Sub-Saharan Africa, and 2 are in South Asia.

In addition, in-depth interviews were conducted with 4 NDFIs to identify good practices. Interviewed NDFIs include the Fideicomisos Instituidos en Relación con la Agricultura (Mexico), the Korea Development Bank, the Türkiye Sinai Kalkinma Bankasi, and the Development Bank of Southern Africa (South Africa), focusing on the four pillars described in the conceptual framework.

## NOTES

1. Notably, the Basel Committee on Banking Supervision recently issued principles for the effective management and supervision of climate-related financial risks, which provides an important baseline for banks' and supervisors' practices related to climate risks.
2. This publication defines *NDFIs* as any type of financial institution that a national government fully or partially owns or controls and that has been given an explicit legal mandate to reach socioeconomic goals in a region, sector, or market segment. Development Banks are the largest NDFIs, but there are other institutions—such as public credit guarantee funds, public trust funds, or public credit agencies—that are included under this definition.
3. This number is based on the Institute of New Structural Economics and Agence Française de Développement Public Developments Bank Database (November 2022).
4. The SOFI diagnostic is conducted in the context of the Integrated State-Owned Enterprise Diagnostic, the Financial Sector Assessment Program, or on a stand-alone basis at the level of the SOFI sector or individual institutions.
5. Assessment of NDFIs' financial performance and economic impact of their green activities is beyond the scope of this publication, which focuses on reviewing NDFI institutional arrangements for green financing. The financial performance assessment would involve assessing profitability in relation to the risk assumed, including climate risks. Evaluating the economic impact of green activities involves assessing contribution to climate goals. The assessment, however, covers whether institutions have systems in place to measure and monitor climate risks in their portfolios and whether they track reduction in carbon emissions. Similarly, the publication does not review the C&E legal framework of the countries in which NDFIs operate or the extent to which the prudential regulatory framework includes environmental or climate considerations. However, the publication covers NDFIs practices to address C&E effects.
6. Based on interviews and consultations, UNDP's report assessed (a) the role of public development banks in scaling financing toward SDGs, (b) the good practices that banks have already developed, and (c) how national and international actors, including MDBs and the United Nations, can support this agenda.

## BIBLIOGRAPHY

de la Torre, A., J. C. Gozzi, and S. L. Schmukler. 2007. *Innovative Experiences in Access to Finance: Market-Friendly Roles for the Visible Hand?* Washington, DC: Latin American Development Forum, World Bank.

Deloitte. 2022. *The Turning Point*. Washington, DC: Deloitte, UNDP, World Bank, and IADB.

Gutierrez, E., and T. Kliatskova. 2021. *National Development FIs: Trends, Crisis Response Activities, and Lessons Learned*. Washington, DC: World Bank.

Gutierrez, E., H. P. Rudolph, T. Homa, and E. Bianco Beneit. 2011. "Development Banks: Role and Mechanisms to Increase Their Efficiency." Policy Research Working Paper WPS 5729, World Bank, Washington, DC.

Hainz, C., and H. Hakenes. 2012. "The Politician and His Banker—How to Efficiently Grant State Aid." *Journal of Public Economics* 96 (1–2): 218–25.

IADB (Inter-American Development Bank). 2021. *A Guidebook for National Development Banks on Climate Risk*.

Johnson, J., G. Ruta, U. Baldos, R. Cervigni, S. Chonabayashi, E. Corong, O. Gavryliuk, J. Gerber, T. Hertel, C. Nootenboom, and S. Polasky. 2021. *The Economic Case for Nature: A Global Earth-Economy Model to Assess Development Policy Pathways*. Washington, DC: World Bank.

Levy-Yeyati, E. L., A. Micco, and U. Panizza. 2004. "Should the Government Be in the Banking Business? The Role of State-Owned and Development Banks." Working Paper 517, Inter-American Development Bank, Washington, DC.

Lütkehermöller, K., A. Kachi, A. Pauthier, and I. Cochran. 2021. *Operationalizing Framework on Aligning with the Paris Agreement*. Washington, DC: Climate Institute.

Rozenberg, J., and M. Fay. 2019. *Beyond the Gap: How Countries Can Afford the Infrastructure They Need While Protecting the Planet*. Washington, DC: World Bank.

UNDP (United Nations Development Programme). 2022. *The Role of Public Development Banks in Scaling Up Sustainable Finance*. New York: UNDP.

World Bank. 2012. *Global Financial Development Report 2013: Rethinking the Role of the State in Finance*. Washington, DC: World Bank.

World Bank. 2022a. *Achieving Climate and Development Goals: The Financing Question*. Washington, DC: World Bank.

World Bank. 2022b. *The Food and Energy Crisis: Weathering the Storm*. Washington, DC: World Bank.

World Bank. 2022c. *GDP (current US$)*. Databank. Washington, DC: World Bank.

World Bank. 2023. *Spending Needs to Address Selected Global Challenge: Background Note for the Evolution Roadmap*. Unpublished manuscript.

# 2 Landscape of NDFIs

## SUMMARY

National Development Financial Institutions (NDFIs) are highly diverse in size, financial performance, development objectives, business models, funding arrangements, and governance practices. The roles that NDFIs can play in the green transition differ widely and largely depend on their specific structure and scope. This chapter provides an overview of the landscape of NDFIs, presenting a general description of their growth trends, key challenges faced by them, and how they may differ by funding source, structure, and mandate across regions.

## BACKGROUND

NDFIs cover a variety of financial institutions (FIs) that are typically state-owned and have a socioeconomic objective. NDFIs have a policy objective that is closely related to the economic development of a country or given sector. Although they may not technically be FIs by country definitions, NDFIs have their own balance sheets independent from the government that typically owns them.[1] Development Financial Institutions (DFIs) include Development Banks (DBs), nonbank institutions that provide credit for developmental purposes (for example, the Fideicomisos Instituidos en Relación con la Agricultura [FIRA] in Mexico or Caisse des Dépôts in France), and partial credit guarantee funds. DBs are DFIs with a banking license, which allows them to collect retail or wholesale deposits and provide credit. National DBs are the most common type of DFIs, which is why these terms are sometimes used interchangeably.

## CORE ACTIVITIES

NDFIs' core activity is lending, and the majority rely on international capital markets for funding. According to the World Bank 2017 survey, the most common source of funding is issuing debt in international capital markets (85 percent), followed by borrowing from other FIs (84 percent), offering official development assistance (77 percent), and issuing debt in local debt markets (75 percent; refer to figure 2.1a) (World Bank 2018). The primary activity of NDFIs is lending, with 10 percent focused exclusively on wholesale loans, 40 percent providing only retail loans, and 50 percent providing a combination of the two. About half of NDFIs provide loans at subsidized rates, which are funded through cheaper lines of credit from donors, budget transfers from the governments, and, to a lesser extent, cross-subsidization from profitable business lines. Apart from credit, NDFIs also offer loan guarantees (55 percent), private equity and venture capital (47 percent), and deposit accounts (44 percent; refer to figure 2.1b).

**FIGURE 2.1**

**NDFI funding sources and services**

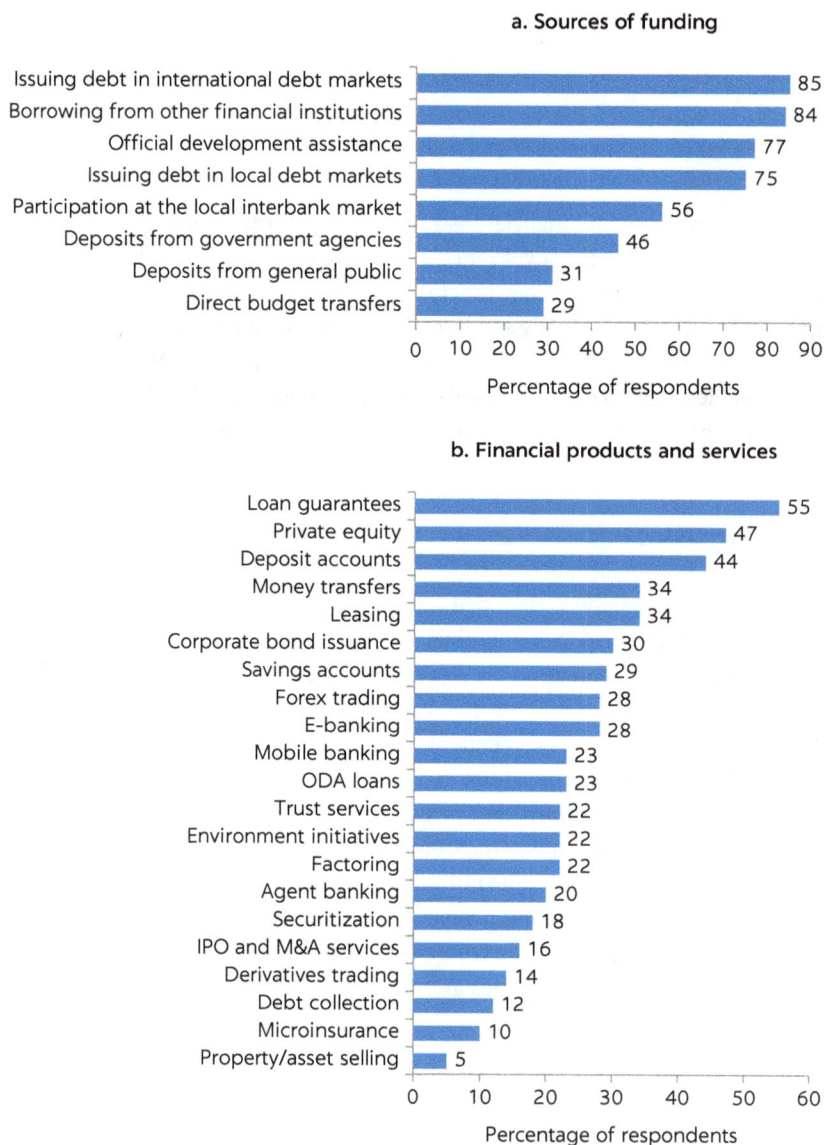

### a. Sources of funding

| Source | Percentage of respondents |
|---|---|
| Issuing debt in international debt markets | 85 |
| Borrowing from other financial institutions | 84 |
| Official development assistance | 77 |
| Issuing debt in local debt markets | 75 |
| Participation at the local interbank market | 56 |
| Deposits from government agencies | 46 |
| Deposits from general public | 31 |
| Direct budget transfers | 29 |

### b. Financial products and services

| Product/Service | Percentage of respondents |
|---|---|
| Loan guarantees | 55 |
| Private equity | 47 |
| Deposit accounts | 44 |
| Money transfers | 34 |
| Leasing | 34 |
| Corporate bond issuance | 30 |
| Savings accounts | 29 |
| Forex trading | 28 |
| E-banking | 28 |
| Mobile banking | 23 |
| ODA loans | 23 |
| Trust services | 22 |
| Environment initiatives | 22 |
| Factoring | 22 |
| Agent banking | 20 |
| Securitization | 18 |
| IPO and M&A services | 16 |
| Derivatives trading | 14 |
| Debt collection | 12 |
| Microinsurance | 10 |
| Property/asset selling | 5 |

*Source:* World Bank 2018.
*Note:* IPO = initial public offering; M&A = mergers and acquisitions; NDFI = National Development Financial Institution; ODA = official development assistance.

## COUNTRIES AND REGIONS

High-income countries (HICs) and upper-middle-income countries (UMICs) alone account for about two-thirds of NDFIs (refer to figure 2.2). Far fewer NDFIs exist in low-income countries (LICs) than in HICs, UMICs, and lower-middle-income countries (LMICs) (refer to figure 2.2a). This fact may be because of difficulties in raising funds for NDFIs (including in capital markets), as well as poor institutional capacity to establish and operate NDFIs. The small market size of LICs may also reduce the need to establish many specialized NDFIs. As shown in figure 2.2b, the largest concentration of national and subnational NDFIs is in the Europe and Central Asia region (102 NDFIs, or 22 percent of total NDFIs). This is followed by East Asia and Pacific (18 percent), Sub-Saharan Africa (17 percent), and Latin America and the Caribbean (17 percent).

## MISSIONS AND MANDATES

About 33 percent of NDFIs have a broad mission of supporting economic and social development. In low-income economies, more than half of the NDFIs

FIGURE 2.2

**Distribution of NDFIs**

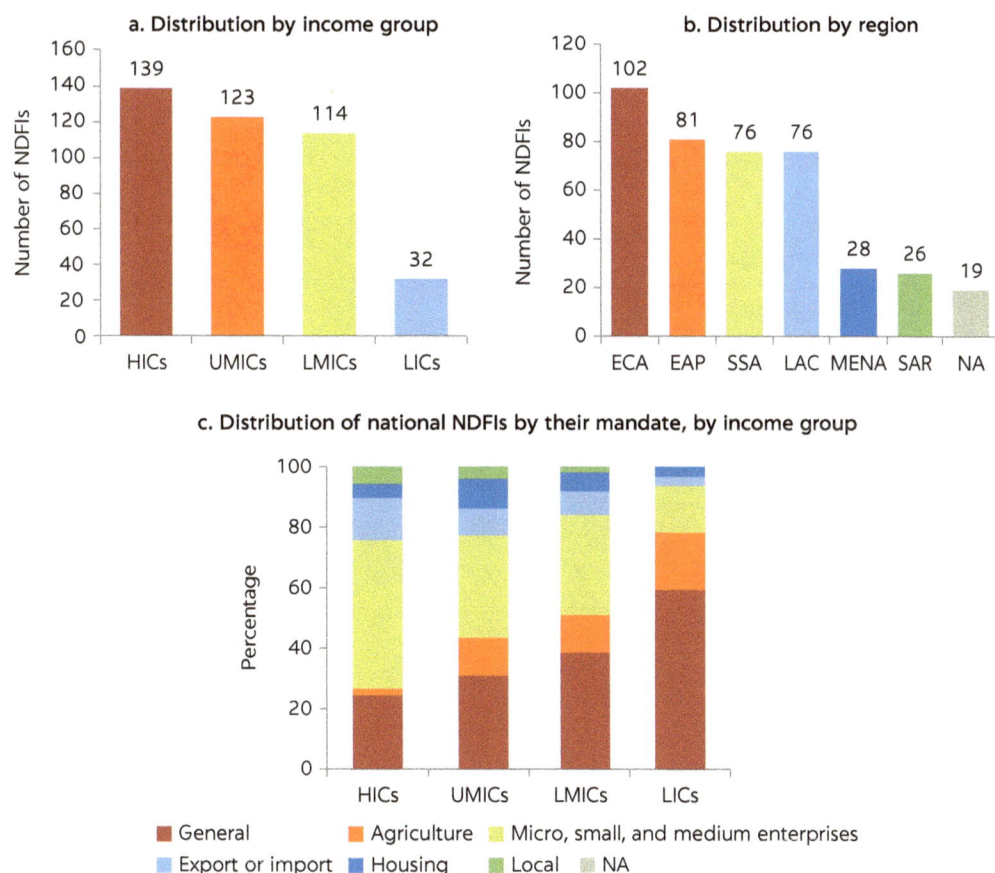

Source: Data based on Xu et al. (2021).
Note: EAP = East Asia and Pacific; ECA = Europe and Central Asia; HIC = high-income country; LAC = Latin America and the Caribbean; LIC = low-income country; LMIC = lower-middle-income country; MENA = Middle East and North Africa; NA = North America; NDFI = National Development Financial Institution; SAR = South Asia; SSA = Sub-Saharan Africa; UMIC = upper-middle-income country.

have a general mandate, whereas NDFIs in HICs have more specific mandates, in part because these countries have more than one NDFI (refer to figure 2.2c). Many NDFIs in HICs, UMICs, and LMICs have a focused mandate to support micro, small, and medium enterprises and entrepreneurship, reaching 49 percent of all NDFIs in high-income economies. In contrast, agriculture banks are much more prevalent in low-income economies.

## NOTE

1. Most NDFIs are government-owned; however, there are some private NDFIs, such as Türkiye Sinai Kalkinma Bankasi (TSKB) in Türkiye or the Green Investment Bank in the United Kingdom, that were created as public development institutions and subsequently were privatized without changing their green focus.

## BIBLIOGRAPHY

Xu, Jiajun, Régis Marodon, Xinshun Ru, Xiaomeng Ren, and Xinyue Wu. 2021. "What Are Public Development Banks and Development Financing Institutions?—Qualification Criteria, Stylized Facts and Development Trends." *China Economic Quarterly International* 1(4): 271–94. Public Development Banks and Development Financing Institutions Database; http://www.dfidatabase.pku.edu.cn/.

World Bank. 2018. *2017 Survey of National Development Banks*. Washington, DC: World Bank.

# 3 State and Trends of Greening NDFIs

## BACKGROUND

To identify lessons learned and best practices of greening National Development Financial Institutions (NDFIs), the World Bank launched a survey in January 2022, as well as conducted in-depth interviews. Responses to the survey were received from 22 NDFIs, with wide geographical and income-level coverage. Appendix A describes the survey methodology.[1] The in-depth interviews were conducted with four NDFIs:

1. Fideicomisos Instituidos en Relación con la Agricultura (FIRA, Mexico),

2. Korea Development Bank (KDB, the Republic of Korea),

3. Türkiye Sinai Kalkinma Bankasi (TSKB, Türkiye), and

4. Development Bank of Southern Africa (DBSA, South Africa).

Appendix B provides more details about the case studies. The assessment framework and recommendations focused on the following:

- Integration of climate and environmental (C&E) considerations into NDFIs' governance and strategies,
- Mobilization of financing toward C&E objectives,
- C&E risk management practices, and
- C&E disclosures and reporting.

## GOVERNANCE AND STRATEGY

Good governance and strategy are key to NDFIs' prioritizing their actions to support C&E objectives and facilitate coordination across different stakeholders, including national and subnational policymakers and sector participants. A good strategy and governance framework should have clearly defined objectives that are in line with country C&E objectives, specify the roles and responsibilities to achieve different objectives, and describe actions to be taken by different actors to ensure the strategy's adequate implementation.

Over 80 percent of the NDFIs surveyed have adopted green objectives, and 73 percent are contributing to the implementation of the Paris Agreement's Nationally Determined Contribution (NDC) targets. Over 80 percent of respondents have set green objectives or prepared a strategy to green their portfolio (refer to figure 3.1). In many cases, green objectives are reflected in the institution's mission and strategy, being accommodated within the previously existing legal mandate.

Green strategies sometimes focus on reducing the NDFIs' own carbon footprint in addition to greening their portfolio (refer to the FIRA case study in appendix B). In most cases, the strategies are published. Seventy-seven percent of respondents reported having made public pledges or commitments to align their activities with international or national climate goals and to be involved in the implementation of the country's NDCs. However, only a few institutions (including the Brazilian Development Bank [BNDES], TSKB, and Kreditanstalt für Wiederaufbau [KFW]) have set targets or disclosed their contributions to NDCs. For example, BNDES has an NDC Panel and discloses its contribution to the Brazilian NDCs online. In addition, KFW has committed to a carbon-neutral portfolio by 2050. Alignment with national climate goals is often supported by adopting a sustainable strategy, being accredited by the Global Climate Fund (GCF), or developing green financing facilities.

The majority of the NDFIs examined have specific green financing targets and exclude from their portfolio the financing of some nongreen projects or sectors. Of the 22 NDFIs surveyed, 15 have green financing targets. Some institutions target the number of transactions for climate objectives or the United Nations Sustainable Development Goals (SDGs), whereas others aim to increase green financing in absolute terms, in the percentage of new commitments, or in the share of green assets in their portfolio. In addition, some institutions target a reduction in financing of polluting sectors, such as fossil fuels; 13 NDFIs reported that they exclude financing of specific nongreen or nonsustainable projects from their portfolio. Most respondents point to exclusion lists of activities in line with national regulations or international standards (for example, KFW refers to the International Finance Corporation [IFC] exclusion list; Banco de Inversión y

FIGURE 3.1

**NDFIs show a high-level commitment to the green agenda**

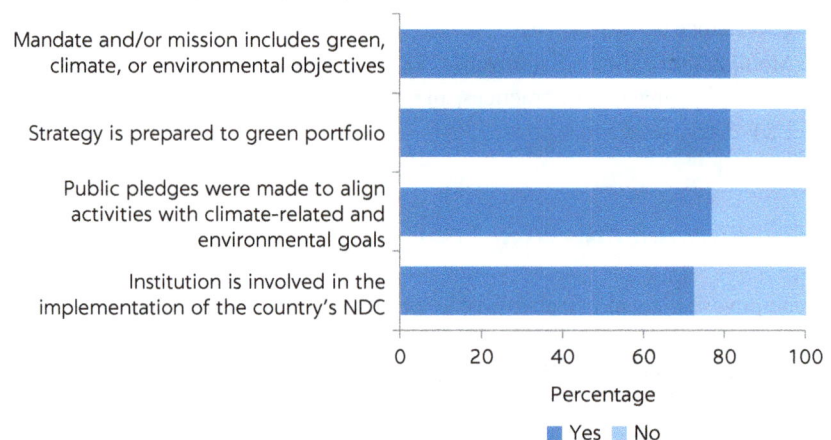

Source: Figure original to this publication based on World Bank data.
Note: NDC = Nationally Determined Contribution; NDFI = National Development Financial Institution.

Comercio Exterior refers to the World Bank and Inter-American Development Bank exclusion lists). A few institutions do not have exclusion lists but instead point to the prohibition against funding coal mining or coal-generated energy (for example, TSKB, KDB, and the Industrial Bank of Korea [IBK]). NDFIs operating through financial intermediaries (second tier) often impose their green financing targets on other financial institutions (FIs). Furthermore, some NDFIs already have binding targets, whereas others impose targets for green financing to be achieved in the future. Some reported that they have more than achieved their green targets.

More than half of NDFIs incorporate C&E considerations into their governance arrangements. The majority have created dedicated units and high-level committees to address C&E topics, often supported by the approval of specific policies and strategies. Thirteen NDFIs incorporate C&E considerations into their governance arrangements. Six did not provide details or refer to the adoption of C&E-related policies implemented by the existing institutional units. The remaining respondents referred to the creation of either specific units assessing and managing the environmental and social impacts of projects and providing sustainable finance or of high-level committees and director positions focused on C&E or sustainability issues more broadly. Examples of good NDFI practices on governance and strategy are presented in box 3.1.

---

**BOX 3.1**

## Good NDFI practices on governance and strategy

NDFIs rarely have C&E–related goals explicitly included in their mandates. For example, FIRA's mandate is "to promote, until it is well established, an inclusive, sustainable and productive agri-food and rural sector." KDB's mandate is to support the country's sustainable growth. Similarly, TSKB's mission focuses on inclusive and sustainable development, and DBSA's Act refers to financing sustainable development projects and programs.

Lack of an explicit legal mandate has not prevented NDFIs from incorporating C&E considerations into their operations or from developing strategies to green their portfolios. FIRA has developed a sustainability strategy with three pillars that (a) aim to avoid environmental harm, (b) finance green projects, and (c) catalyze support for green financing. KDB's green financing strategy's goal is to support the government's NDC and 2050 carbon neutrality target. TSKB published the Combating Climate Change and Adaptation Policy in June 2020. In 2021, DBSA approved the Just Transition Investment Framework to become a net-zero bank by 2050. KDB and TSKB have also phased out their investments in coal-powered energy. NDFIs have indicated that formal inclusion of green objectives in their mandates may give them more legitimacy and clout to make progress on these topics.

Institutions with green or sustainability strategies often set green financing targets and track green financing. FIRA developed a taxonomy to label green financing products, and DBSA uses the International Development Finance Club taxonomy. KDB developed a sustainable framework aligned with international standards, and TSKB tracks financing linked to climate and SDGs. KDB's aim is to increase the share of green financing to 16.8 percent of its total annual financing by 2030. TSKB has set a target of a 60 percent share of C&E-focused or SDG-linked loans in the total portfolio by 2025.

Some institutions have created high-level committees in charge of the development and implementation of C&E policies. For example, BNDES has a Sustainability Committee linked to the bank's Executive Board, which is the main forum for discussing C&E considerations. Its board of directors has a subcommittee dealing with ESG aspects. In addition, the bank has assigned a director responsible for the subject in the institution, a sustainability team in the strategic planning division, and an environment department.

*continued*

**Box 3.1,** *continued*

In addition, IBK has established its ESG committee as the top decision-making organization under the board of directors, which regularly reviews and makes resolutions for risk, opportunities, and strategies related to climate change based on international standards. Furthermore, the higher decision-making body of FIRA, the Technical Committee, has become involved in environmental issues, reflecting its signing of the Sustainability Protocol of the Mexican Bank Association, which includes a governance principle that indicates that the higher decision-making bodies of financial institutions should be involved in C&E issues. FIRA has also created a high-level working group that comprises all the different areas in the bank involved in climate issues. Finally, TSKB's sustainability strategy, vision and goals, and climate-related risks and opportunities are addressed by the Sustainability Committee with the active participation of the board of directors and the Executive Committee.

*Note:* BNDES = Brazilian Development Bank; C&E = climate and environmental; DBSA = Development Bank of Southern Africa (South Africa); ESG = environmental, social, and governance; FIRA = Fideicomisos Instituidos en Relación con la Agricultura (Mexico); IBK = Industrial Bank of Korea (the Republic of Korea); KDB = Korea Development Bank (the Republic of Korea); NDC = Nationally Determined Contribution; NDFI = National Development Financial Institution; SDG = Sustainable Development Goal; TSKB = Türkiye Sinai Kalkinma Bankasi.

## GREEN FINANCING SOURCES AND USES

Countries face a significant financing gap in reaching their climate goals. The first batch of Country Climate and Development Reports from the World Bank found that the financing needed for climate action across the 24 countries analyzed will average 1.4 percent of gross domestic product (GDP) by 2030. However, large differences exist across country income classes: 1.1 percent of GDP, on average, in upper-middle-income countries, increasing to 5.1 percent in lower-middle-income countries and 8 percent in low-income countries (LICs) (World Bank 2023). These data suggest that climate-development financing needs are a significantly larger percentage of GDP in countries that have contributed the least to global warming and where access to capital markets and private capital is more limited.

NDFIs, which could help close this financing gap, have an important position in the domestic financing landscape given their proximity to policymakers, local markets, and international development finance. They are also unique in that they can potentially deploy affordable, flexible, and risk-tolerant funding tailored to country context, thus addressing key market barriers that impede private investments for climate action.

NDFIs are already leading players in climate financing, especially in LICs and middle-income countries (MICs). According to the Climate Policy Initiative (CPI), the annual average climate financing provided by NDFIs in 2019–20 was US$145 billion, or 22 percent of total climate financing, representing the majority of public climate financing during that period (refer to figure 3.2a).[2] This situation is especially true for LICs and MICs, where more than 60 percent of annual average 2019–20 climate financing was provided by public actors, led by NDFIs (45 percent), state-owned FIs (17 percent), and multilateral Development Financial Institutions (DFIs) (17 percent). By regional distribution, the East Asia and Pacific region (75 percent; refer to figure 3.2b) receives the most climate financing from NDFIs by far. The annual average flows tagged to adaptation in

FIGURE 3.2

**NDFI climate financing sources and regional distribution, global annual averages, 2019–20**

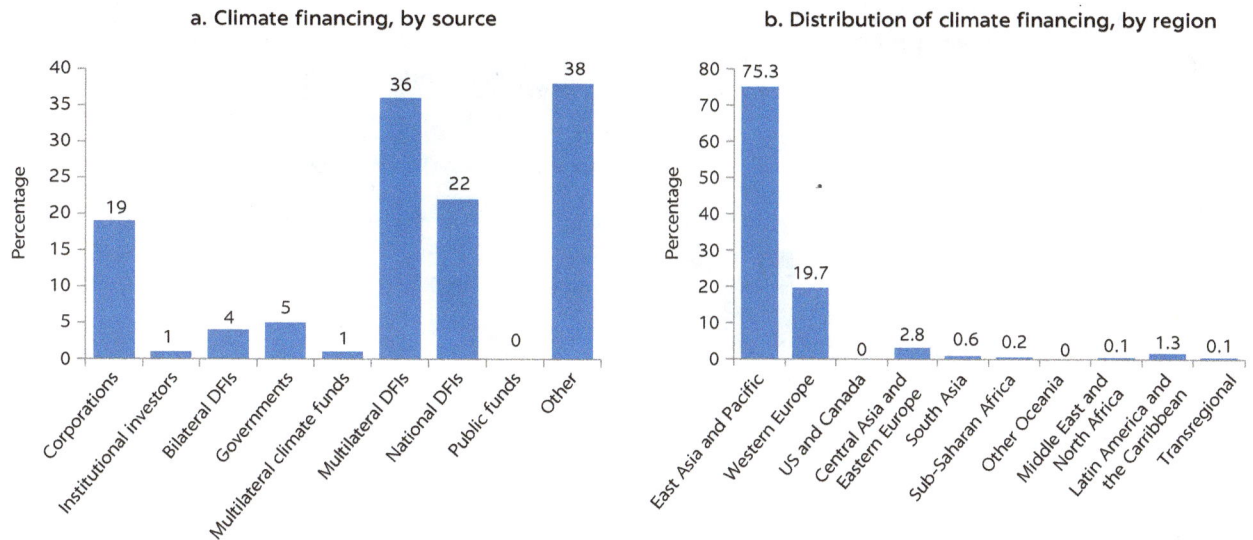

a. Climate financing, by source

b. Distribution of climate financing, by region

*Source:* Climate Policy Initiative (CPI 2022).
*Note:* DFI = Development Financial Institution; NDFI = National Development Financial Institution.

LICs and MICs in 2019–20 were about US$44 billion (that is, approximately 10 percent of total climate financing flows).[3] Almost all adaptation financing tracked to LICs and MICs was provided by public actors (98 percent), such as multilateral DFIs (37 percent of public adaptation finance in LICs and MICs) and national DFIs (34 percent).[4]

Nevertheless, the survey results suggest that the share of green assets in NDFIs' credit portfolios is still relatively low (approximately 14 percent, on average), and the majority of investment is in climate mitigation projects. The share of green assets differs substantially between institutions. Of the 12 surveyed NDFIs that reported the share of their credit portfolio in green assets, 7 have a modest share of green assets below 10 percent, 4 have a share of green assets between 10 percent and 25 percent, and in only 1 does the share of green assets exceed 50 percent of the total portfolio (refer to figure 3.3a).

Most of the NDFIs do not distinguish between financing for climate adaptation and that for climate mitigation. Some NDFIs are, however, developing methodologies to identify what could be considered climate adaptation and mitigation financing. The NDFIs with mitigation and adaptation projects have a share of their portfolio in adaptation that is substantially lower than that for mitigation. In addition, some NDFIs provide financing exclusively for mitigation purposes. The bias toward mitigation investments is further evidenced in other studies, such as that of the International Development Finance Club (IDFC), which suggests that US$146 billion of the US$185 billion in green financing provided by IDFC members in 2020 was dedicated to climate mitigation (IDFC 2021). CPI data similarly show that approximately 89 percent of climate financing from NDFIs is dedicated to climate mitigation (CPI 2022).

The survey results also suggest that NDFI's green financing is concentrated in selected sectors, with the majority in the power, agriculture, transport, and industry sectors (refer to figure 3.3b). Of the 22 NDFIs surveyed, 17 provide

**FIGURE 3.3**

## NDFIs' survey responses on green financing practices

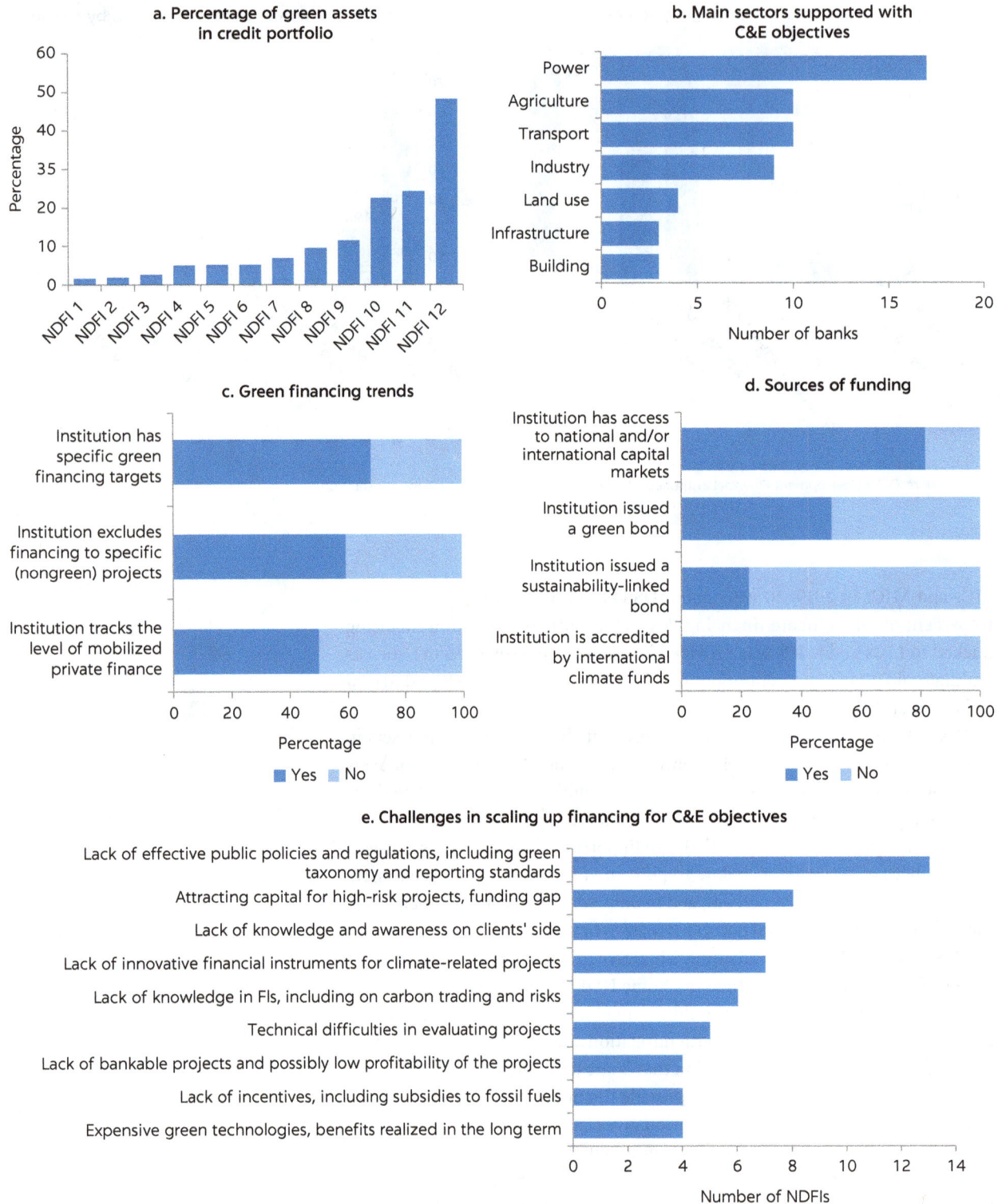

### a. Percentage of green assets in credit portfolio

### b. Main sectors supported with C&E objectives

### c. Green financing trends

### d. Sources of funding

### e. Challenges in scaling up financing for C&E objectives

*Source:* Figure original to this publication based on World Bank data.
*Note:* Panel a shows the results for 12 NDFIs that provided responses to this survey question. C&E = climate and environmental; FI = financial institution; NDFI = National Development Financial Institution.

financing to renewable energy projects, such as hydropower and solar projects. NDFIs also finance sustainable transport (10 NDFIs), including electric and alternative-fuel vehicles, as well as sustainable agriculture and farming (10 NDFIs). Some institutions also provide financing for green infrastructure projects, water efficiency, waste management, and pollution prevention, as well as sustainable tourism.

NDFIs' main clients range from national and subnational governments to large corporations, including state-owned enterprises. In addition, some NDFIs provide financing to micro, small, and medium enterprises (MSMEs), farmers and small agri-producers, and entrepreneurs and individuals. The banks that provide second-tier lending provide financing to the above-mentioned groups via other bank and nonbank FIs.

The survey and stakeholder consultations found that NDFIs use a wide range of FIs to channel green financing. The most widely used instrument to provide green financing is lending. NDFIs provide first- and second-tier lending, with short- to long-term loans and credit lines.[5] Less than 25 percent of institutions reported providing concessional climate financing, although this figure may be underrepresented. Only four institutions reported pricing as part of their portfolio at concessional terms, and the subsidy applied to more than half of the portfolio in only one case. Three institutions indicated that the information was not available, and others did not consider the concessional financing received.

Some NDFIs provide credit guarantees to finance green projects, and some also issue grants, particularly to underserved segments. Less widely used instruments include equity investment financing, venture financing, and project structuring. Apart from financial products, some NDFIs provide technical assistance and advisory services to help clients green their activities.

Some NDFIs mobilize private financing for green projects, but more could be done. A few institutions also established mechanisms to track and monitor how much private financing was mobilized (refer to figure 3.3c). In addition, for some NDFI projects, contribution from the private sector is mandatory at some percentage of the project value. However, the focus on private finance mobilization seems limited, and its potential is largely unexplored. Several NDFIs also collaborate with subnational development banks to channel financing to the local level. In addition, NDFIs sometimes have requirements to co-finance projects with other FIs (for example, Mexican NDFIs have co-financing requirements for renewable-energy projects).

Eighteen out of 22 NDFIs have access to international or national capital markets, but the use of green debt instruments has not yet been mainstreamed (refer to figure 3.3d). Only half of the respondents have issued a green bond, and less than a quarter have issued a sustainability-linked bond. Nevertheless, it is important to note that, in several cases, NDFIs were first movers in green bond issuance. For example, Nacional Financiera issued the first Mexican green bond in 2015 (and was the first in Latin America to have climate bond certification). Less than 40 percent have accreditation to access international climate funds such as the GCF. Many NDFIs do not use the resources even if they are accredited. Examples of good practices on sources and uses for green financing are presented in box 3.2.

The key challenge to scaling up financing for C&E objectives is the lack of effective public policies and regulations. Thirteen of 20 banks indicated that the

## Good NDFI practices on green financing sources and uses

Some NDFIs have developed specialized programs and products for financing of C&E objectives and prioritized projects that are not commercially viable. For example, FIRA has developed the Pro-Sostenible Program, which provides an interest rate subsidy (cash back) to final borrowers of sustainable projects using donor funding. The Energy Efficiency Program provides a technological guarantee, paying the difference between estimated and realized savings from the adoption of energy-efficient technologies. TSKB is currently developing various thematic credit lines (projects) with topics related to the circular economy, green deal promotion, climate change adaptation, and employment creation via green growth. KDB has targeted projects that are not commercially viable, such as early-stage investments in nascent technology solutions (for example, carbon capture and storage, green hydrogen).

NDFIs, often in collaboration with other national entities, provide credit enhancement mechanisms for green financing. For example, the National Forest Fund and the Credit Guarantee Fund for the Efficient Use of Water, co-administered by FIRA, offer credit guarantees to financial intermediaries, with a higher guarantee for sustainable projects (65 percent versus the standard 40–50 percent guarantee) at no additional cost. Moreover, KDB utilizes funding from the Green Climate Fund to cover first losses of private sector green investments. KDB also lowers interest rates for certain green projects to increase the attractiveness of these investments. Finally,

DBSA has launched the Climate Finance Facility, which focuses on blended finance mechanisms and credit enhancements, such as subordinated debt and tenor extensions.

NDFIs also provide nonfinancial support to borrowers in relation to green financing. For example, the PROINFOR Program, administered by FIRA, supports small forest producers with technical assistance to adopt sustainable production practices. In addition, TSKB via Escarus (TSKB Sustainability Consultancy) provides technical assistance and consultancy services, such as thematic bond issuances, to its clients. Finally, DBSA provides project preparation support to further facilitate the development of green bankable projects.

NDFIs often catalyze development of local green financing markets by raising the profile and demonstrating the feasibility of green bonds with potential issuers. For example, KDB was a first mover in a green bond market in the Republic of Korea that currently accounts for ₩3.7 trillion (equivalent to US$3 billion) of green bonds issued up to March 2022. KDB further bolsters the private sector's participation in the labeled bond market by arranging, underwriting, and investing in green and sustainable bonds. KDB has issued three primary collateralized bond obligations backed by privately placed ESG bonds issued by MSMEs that back corporate capital investments in green projects, extending the reach to MSMEs and private placements.

*Note:* C&E = climate and environmental; DBSA = Development Bank of Southern Africa (South Africa); ESG = environmental, social, and governance; FIRA = Fideicomisos Instituidos en Relación con la Agricultura (Mexico); KDB = Korea Development Bank (the Republic of Korea); MSME = micro, small, and medium enterprise; NDFI = National Development Financial Institution; TSKB = Türkiye Sinai Kalkinma Bankasi.

lack of an enabling policy environment is a major barrier to attracting public and private capital for climate projects. For example, enabling policies can include a common green taxonomy, as well as disclosure and reporting standards, that allows for transparent identification and monitoring of green financing flows. Strengthening national climate strategies and legislation are also required to signal the government's long-term commitment to the climate agenda. In addition, policies that encourage public-private partnerships are important to encourage collaboration on green investments between NDFIs and the private sector.

Funding gaps, particularly in LICs and MICs, are another challenge NDFIs face. Eight NDFIs indicated that it is difficult to attract capital for high-risk, long-term projects; many NDFIs have limited access to funding because their local capital markets are underdeveloped, and they have no access to international capital markets. Accessing concessional financing from global financing mechanisms such as the GCF is a long process, with provisions that can be challenging to implement. In addition, this issue exposes banks to the risk of foreign exchange rates and requires implementing costly hedging mechanisms. Furthermore, available patient capital (for example, equity funds, private angels) is lacking for green projects. Some NDFIs indicated that financial incentives in the form of government guarantees might be useful to address funding gaps.

Several NDFIs indicated that the lack of knowledge and awareness of C&E issues is a further challenge. NDFIs revealed that they have limited knowledge and competences on topics related to green financing, such as project structuring, financing instruments, carbon trading, and evaluation of C&E risks, and require capacity building, specialized training, and knowledge sharing to be more aware of international best practices. In addition, clients often lack awareness and knowledge, according to seven NDFIs surveyed. MSMEs and the general population generally are unaware of key issues such as environmental problems or energy-saving benefits, which hampers demand. Awareness and promotional campaigns can help create demand for green technologies. Moreover, some companies, especially MSMEs, have limited knowledge and lack the technical personnel to implement green projects.

Several other barriers exist to scaling up green financing, including project complexities and cost, a lack of incentives, and tailored financial solutions. Some NDFIs indicated that costs for project preparation and implementation are high (refer to figure 3.3e). Therefore, high real and perceived implementation costs might further suppress demand. Identification and technical evaluation of green projects at the preparation stage often is costly, requires specialized skills, and is compounded by the lack of transparent information and data. Supervision and impact evaluation of such projects is also more costly than that for other projects.

In addition, green projects (for example, hydropower, biodiversity) are long term by nature and have a high risk, with their benefits realized only after project completion. Smaller-scale projects that have greater sustainability value often have a lower internal rate of return, as well as complex, costly transactions and institutional arrangements. These additional costs put green projects at a disadvantage, decreasing the willingness of the private sector to provide financing.

Some NDFIs also highlighted the lack of incentives, such as economic, financial, and legal, to provide financing to green projects. In some countries, subsidies for fossil fuels can set negative economic incentives for climate mitigation projects (for example, renewable energy). Seven NDFIs highlighted the importance of developing innovative financial instruments (such as blended financing) or de-risking instruments (such as guarantees) that are specifically customized for climate-related and environmental projects.

The surveyed NDFIs identified several priorities for scaling up financing to meet C&E objectives in the next 1–5 years. The NDFIs plan to focus on obtaining access to funding to finance green projects, such as improving access to concessional resources, including from the GCF; mobilizing private financing; and tapping into the labeled bond market. Several NDFIs are working to set up partnerships and collaborations and to coordinate with key stakeholders and potential funding agencies to scale green financing efforts.

In addition, NDFIs also plan to enhance demand for green projects by raising awareness through building campaigns and educating clients, as well as by bringing to the market new financial products targeting certain groups of customers and projects. For example, BNDES aims to scale BNDES environmental, social, and governance (ESG) credit, which provides a discount on funding to borrowers attaining certain sustainability-linked objectives. Some institutions mentioned the need to engage with borrowers to reduce their carbon footprint.

## C&E FINANCIAL RISK MANAGEMENT

C&E risk management practices in the financial sector have evolved substantially over the past decade. An increasing number of central banks and regulators are taking action globally to address the impacts of C&E physical and transition risks on the stability of FIs and their financial systems. Standard-setting bodies, as well as the Network of Central Banks and Supervisors for Greening the Financial System, have started to issue guidance for regulators and FIs on how to manage C&E risks, including a recent set of principles for the banking sector issued by the Basel Committee on Banking Supervision (BCBS).

In response to this guidance, FIs have begun to integrate climate and, in some cases, broader environmental financial risks into their risk management frameworks and strategies. This approach is different from the environmental and social risk management (ESRM) assessments that NDFIs and other institutions have historically conducted to consider the impact of their financing activities on environmental and social issues.

The following section considers C&E risks primarily from the financial risk angle, given that a well-established foundation for ESRM already exists.[6] Although ESRM primarily looks at the external impact of operations, in certain cases, this examination could also translate into financial risks (primarily credit risk) or reputational risks. Sometimes the two approaches are part of one broad C&E risk management framework.

In general, our survey (see figure 3.4) suggests that the integration of C&E financial risks in NDFIs' strategies is limited. The consideration of these risks generally is not incorporated into long-term organizational strategies. Even though nearly three-quarters of the NDFIs indicated that they have integrated some C&E considerations into their strategy, these considerations are often high level (from a general sustainability perspective) rather than a more in-depth analysis of the impact of long-term C&E financial risks on their business.

NDFIs recognize the relevance of C&E financial risks for their business models, but, in most cases, they do not expect them to materialize in the short term. Nearly all (86 percent) of the NDFIs surveyed expect that C&E financial risks will affect their business model. However, these NDFIs stated that these risks are generally not expected to materialize over the short term, although several NDFIs—most of which are involved in the agriculture sector—indicated that some risks are already becoming apparent. For example, institutions cited the impact of climate-related weather events on farmers' ability to repay their debts. Other NDFIs noted the impact of changes in precipitation patterns, which triggered financial losses and restructurings for hydropower projects. Depending on the nature and scope of their business models, some NDFIs (for example, those that focus on the agriculture sector) expect climate physical risks to be the main source of risk, whereas other NDFIs (for example, those that focus on fossil fuel industries) indicate that climate transition would be the main source of risk to their business models if they do not adapt to market and regulatory developments that support the low-carbon transition.

FIGURE 3.4

## Survey responses on C&E risk management practices

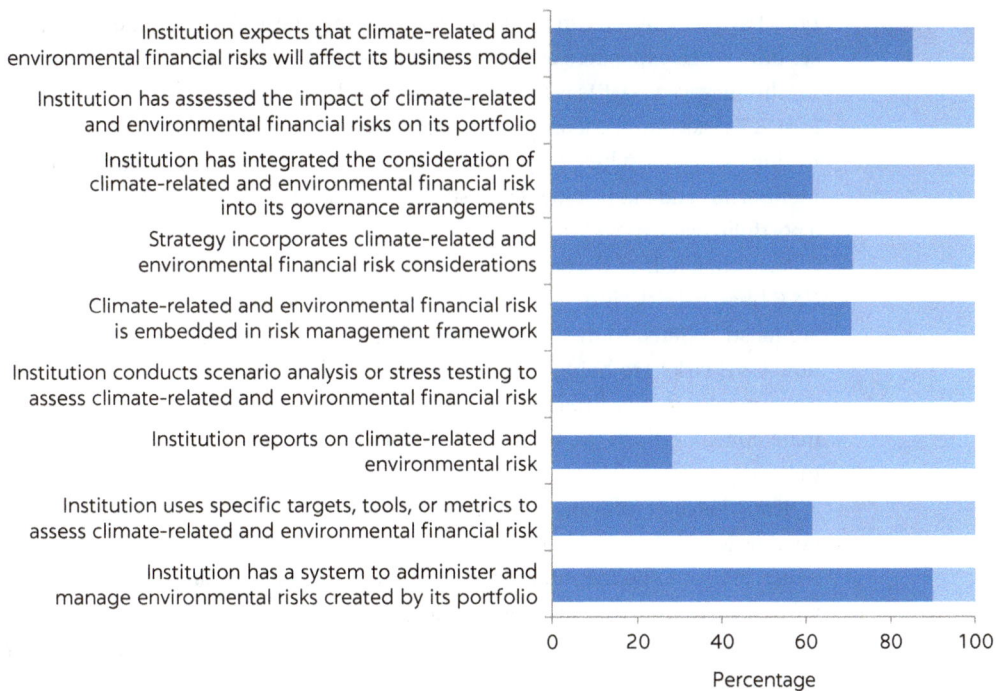

*Source:* Figure original to this publication based on World Bank data.
*Note:* C&E = climate and environmental.

Many NDFIs consider only how their activities impact C&E factors, often as part of ESRM, and do not yet consider how C&E risks translate into financial risks for their own investment and credit portfolio. Less than half of the NDFIs surveyed demonstrate an understanding of the classification of C&E physical and transition risks or their transmission channels to existing categories of prudential financial risk, primarily credit risk. Many institutions see these risks exclusively through the ESRM lens. Ninety percent of the NDFIs have a system in place to assess and manage environmental risks from the impact perspective. This system often is combined with that for social risks as part of broader ESRM systems. In this context, several institutions mentioned the application of environmental safeguards or alignment with, for example, the IFC's Environmental and Social Performance Standards. Therefore, environmental risk is considered more likely at the point of loan origination (considering adverse environmental impacts) rather than at the portfolio level.

Although awareness of the potential implications of C&E financial risks seems high, less than half of the surveyed NDFIs have started assessing the exposure of their portfolio to these risks. Several NDFIs mentioned that they have assessed these risks as part of their ESRM system, although this system may use a different methodology than that for a prudential financial risk assessment. C&E risk assessment methodologies that were mentioned are so far primarily focused on high-level sectoral or geographical exposure assessments or the carbon footprint of the portfolio (for example, refer to the TSKB and DBSA case studies in appendix B for an illustration of risk assessment methodologies).

Only a quarter of NDFIs have started more advanced stress-testing or scenario analysis exercises. However, many institutions indicated that they are looking to develop these capabilities soon, ideally with financial and technical support from multilateral and development partners in this area. Some institutions have set a minimum threshold for assessing these risks, conducting analyses only when exposures exceed a certain value. Moving forward, a top priority for the surveyed NDFIs is to develop methodologies and processes for integrating C&E risks into the loan evaluation, internal rating, loan allocation, and monitoring processes, which may allow NDFIs to also strengthen the identification, monitoring, and management of institutional exposure to potential C&E risks on a portfolio basis.

Less than half of the surveyed NDFIs provided details on the integration of C&E financial risks into their governance arrangements. Governance structures are mostly related to the broader ESRM framework, with less consideration of how C&E risks are being embedded into (credit) risk committee structures. Governance often is different for banks with an agricultural focus, for which climate considerations are more formally embedded in risk management structures or processes.

Knowledge of relevant international standards and frameworks is low. Most notably, NDFIs have limited awareness of the BCBS Principles on climate risks, which are set to be the international baseline standard for addressing climate-related risks in corporate governance, internal controls, risk management, monitoring and reporting, and scenario analysis. Only one NDFI mentioned that these principles are informing the integration of climate risk into its own frameworks and activities. Examples of good NDFI practices for C&E risk management are provided in box 3.3.

Lack of data and standardized methodologies were identified as key challenges hindering NDFIs' ability to mainstream C&E risk management practices. So far,

---

**BOX 3.3**

## Good NDFI practices for C&E risk management

The case studies in appendix B demonstrate an increasing awareness of the urgency and relevance of C&E financial risks to institutions' portfolios and business models. NDFIs have a solid grasp of physical and transition risk concepts, whereas they focus on the impact angle of broader ESRM.

A diversity in approaches exists, with the four NDFI case studies showcasing different innovations and good practices. These encouraging developments could provide an example for other NDFIs looking to develop their capabilities on C&E financial risks. For example, FIRA participated in several pilots, including in a drought stress-testing tool to assess the implications for the risk profile of its loan portfolio and in a study to identify physical risks in its credit portfolio based on climate models and scenarios of the Intergovernmental Panel on Climate Change. Pilots

can be an effective mechanism for institutions to test relevant approaches and develop capacity.

Despite globally recognized data challenges related to measuring Scope 3 emissions, TSKB has taken the ambitious step to calculate and publish the Scope 3 emissions of companies it has financed that operate in carbon-intensive industries. Furthermore, TSKB identifies climate-related risks in its portfolio through a sector-based heat map that will be used as a basis for the development of more advanced scenario analysis and stress-testing approaches that are currently under development.

Particularly noteworthy is the innovative approach KDB has developed to set a capital buffer for transition risk within its 2022 risk management framework. The capital buffer was established by calculating a stressed climate probability of default based on a

*continued*

**Box 3.3,** *continued*

transition risk stress test using the Network for Greening the Financial System scenario to achieve net-zero by 2050.

On the impact side, DBSA has systematically embedded the consideration of environmental risks across all stages of the loan life cycle. This includes the development of its own internal carbon footprinting tool to assess its counterparties. Also recognizing that building up further internal capabilities for the assessment of C&E financial risks is key, DBSA is engaging with numerous relevant networks to develop the required expertise.

*Note:* C&E = climate and environmental; DBSA = Development Bank of Southern Africa (South Africa); ESRM = environmental and social risk management; FIRA = Fideicomisos Instituidos en Relación con la Agricultura (Mexico); KDB = Korea Development Bank (the Republic of Korea); NDFI = National Development Financial Institution; TSKB = Türkiye Sinai Kalkinma Bankasi.

little risk quantification has occurred. NDFIs cited the lack of reliable and high-quality data as a key reason for climate change not being part of their risk management processes. This issue also includes the difficulty of incorporating qualitative data into risk assessment models. One main difficulty in measuring climate risks is that historical data are not reliable indicators for future risks and can weaken predictability. The absence of standards or a harmonized approach to assess C&E financial risk constitutes another barrier to developing an approach to address this risk. Disclosure and reporting standards will also be vital to provide the transparency and information needed to identify, assess, and price the risk.

Other commonly cited challenges are the limited capacity and technical skills within the institution. Several NDFIs highlighted that they have limited internal know-how to allow them to properly address C&E risks, and that risk analyses, including stress testing and scenario analysis, are particularly challenging. Nonconducive regulatory frameworks, or uncertainties about the regulatory direction or emerging regulations, also can impact the assessment of C&E financial risks.

## C&E DISCLOSURES AND REPORTING

Adequate disclosure and reporting are needed to help NDFIs understand, price, and manage C&E risks and green financing opportunities in their portfolios and operations. A growing number of countries have introduced climate and ESG disclosure and reporting requirements for financial and nonfinancial entities. The International Financial Reporting Standards' International Sustainability Standards Board is also in the process of developing a global baseline for sustainability-related disclosure standards, with the goal of providing investors with information about companies' ESG risks and opportunities. Beyond regulatory requirements, many companies already are enhancing their climate or ESG disclosures based on the recommendations of voluntary initiatives such as the Financial Stability Board's Task Force on Climate-Related Financial Disclosures (TCFD) and the Carbon Disclosure Project.

At the same time, several countries have developed green and sustainable taxonomies to uniformly determine what economic activities can be considered environmentally and socially sustainable. A taxonomy can perform a variety of functions, including support financial actors to make informed decisions on sustainable investments, facilitate reliable and comparable disclosures, and provide a consistent way to track what green activities are being financed.

C&E disclosure practices are still at a nascent stage. Some of the surveyed NDFIs have public sustainability reports, but most of these reports do not explicitly cover C&E financial risks. While one-third of the surveyed NDFIs report on C&E financial risks, only one has issued a formal disclosure in line with the TCFD (see the TSKB case study in appendix B). However, several institutions indicated that they are planning to issue TCFD disclosures in the future.

Few NDFIs use tools or metrics to assess the risks related to C&E issues. Some mentioned that they are using greenhouse gas (GHG)–related metrics to assess the carbon sensitivity of their portfolio, although they are not yet planning to publicly disclose this information. Most NDFIs are not collecting specific data to assess C&E financial risks. The main data to inform assessments is related to GHG emissions to advise transition risk analyses, but data are also collected from external parties such as meteorological institutes to support the physical risk assessment.

NDFIs use different classification systems to identify green projects, and many do not disclose green financing volumes publicly, which creates challenges in tracking the amount of green financing provided. Approximately 80 percent of the surveyed NDFIs indicate that they have developed a classification system to identify green projects (refer to figure 3.5). However, these methodologies can vary significantly. Some NDFIs use classification systems developed internationally (for example, IDFC) to identify green projects. Others have developed internal tagging criteria using national or subnational taxonomies. While some banks tag their projects or loans as "green," others use alternative tagging, such as "SDG projects," "NDC projects," and "environment protection projects" (see case studies in appendix B).

For NDFIs without a tagging system in place, work has been kick-started to develop a classification system; however, these frameworks remain works in progress. Based on the developed classification systems, approximately 70 percent of the surveyed NDFIs measure green financing volumes in their portfolio (refer to figure 3.5). Some measure their green financing volumes based on the sources of funds only, possibly underestimating their total green portfolio. Although some NDFIs track their green financing portfolio regularly (monthly, yearly), others perform only one-time assessments.

FIGURE 3.5

**Tracking NDFIs' green financing**

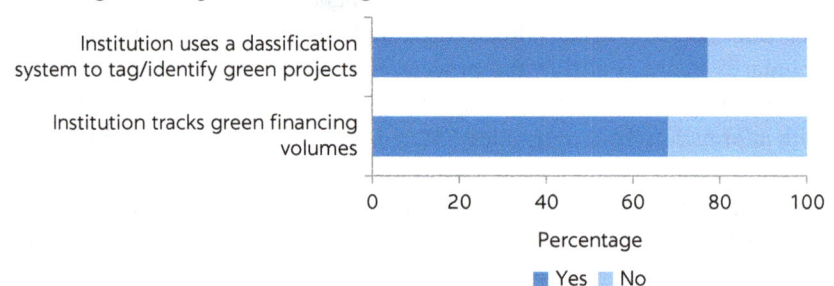

*Source:* Figure original to this publication based on World Bank data.
*Note:* NDFI = National Development Financial Institution.

BOX 3.4

## Good NDFI practices on C&E disclosures and reporting

NDFIs often use internationally recognized methodologies as well as technical assistance from international organizations to develop their green reporting methodologies. For example, DBSA has recently completed a "Green Deep Dive" to obtain a more detailed understanding of its loan book using the methodology of the IDFC. FIRA has developed its taxonomy to track green financing volumes and is now in the process of developing a methodology to identify what could be considered climate adaptation financing with the support of the Agence Française de Développement.

NDFIs disclose their climate-related risks to some extent, with many aiming to start reporting in line with TCFD recommendations. In 2021, TSKB issued its first climate risk report prepared in line with TCFD recommendations that are good practices for reporting. KDB has published annual reports on its implementation of the Equator Principles since 2018 in which they disclose their ESRM processes and projects' exposure to environmental and social risks. FIRA reports all sustainability-related information in the "Memorias de Sostenibilidad," following the Global Standards for Sustainability Reporting.

*Note:* C&E = climate and environmental; DBSA = Development Bank of Southern Africa (South Africa); ESRM = environmental and social risk management; FIRA = Fideicomisos Instituidos en Relación con la Agricultura (Mexico); IDFC = International Development Finance Club; KDB = Korea Development Bank (the Republic of Korea); NDFI = National Development Financial Institution; TCFD = Task Force on Climate-Related Financial Disclosures; TSKB = Türkiye Sinai Kalkinma Bankasi.

Furthermore, many NDFIs do not disclose their green financing volumes publicly. Examples of good NDFI practices on C&E disclosures and reporting are reported in box 3.4.

## NOTES

1.  The results are not necessarily representative for the whole universe of NDFIs, as development financial institutions that did not participate in the survey might be less active in the green financing space. Instead, the results are used to showcase the best practices of NDFIs in developing and pursuing a green agenda.
2.  According to CPI (2022), *NDFIs* are defined as institutions that are owned by a single country and that direct financing domestically. CPI's data source for NDFIs is based on surveys, NDFIs' annual reports or websites, and external sources such as Convergence, BloombergNEF, and the Organisation for Economic Co-operation and Development. Further details on CPI's data collection approach can be found in CPI's methodology note (CPI 2022).
3.  In the reference data set from CPI (2022), the Republic of Korea and Japan are included in the East Asia and Pacific region. In the absence of more granular data for these countries, we use LICs and MICs to mean East Asia and Pacific (including Korea and Japan), Eastern Europe and Central Asia, Latin America and Caribbean, Middle East and North Africa, Sub-Saharan Africa, and South Asia. The financing flows to LICs and MICs are, therefore, overestimated, as they include flows to Korea and Japan.
4.  Adaptation financing is difficult to track because of a lack of widely accepted and consistent definitions and because funds earmarked for adaptation often are internalized as contingencies or risk management expenses by public and private sector actors.
5.  *First-tier lending* is directly to the final borrower (that is, business or individual). *Second-tier lending* is provided to financial intermediaries to later lend to the final borrowers.
6.  This includes through the International Finance Corporation's Environmental and Social Performance Standards, World Bank Environmental and Social Safeguard Policies, the Equator Principles, and NDFIs' internal ESRM policies and standards.

## BIBLIOGRAPHY

CPI (Climate Policy Initiative). 2022. *Global Landscape of Climate Finance: A Decade of Data*. Washington, DC: CPI.

IDFC (International Development Finance Club). 2021. *IDFC Green Finance Mapping Report 2021*. Paris, France: IDFC.

World Bank. 2023. *What You Need to Know about How CCDRs Estimate Climate Finance Needs*. Washington, DC: World Bank.

# 4 Toolkits for Greening NDFIs

## BACKGROUND

The toolkits described in this chapter highlight the range of approaches that National Development Financial Institutions (NDFIs) could take to promote green financing and to manage climate and environmental (C&E) risks. These toolkits are high level, so the implementation of these practical recommendations may differ depending on the local context. For example, the actions taken may depend on an NDFI's level of expertise and commitment to C&E issues, as well as the nature and scope of its business model.

In some cases, it may be more effective to apply different toolkits together in a package. In other cases, NDFIs may prefer a phased approach, starting with a selected toolkit. In addition, whether NDFIs can successfully green their operations may depend on factors that are beyond their control.

## GOVERNANCE AND STRATEGY

NDFIs should develop an internal strategy to identify key priorities for managing C&E opportunities and risks, modifying institutional mandates or missions as necessary. Developing an institutional strategy to address C&E issues is essential for NDFIs to initiate their green transformation. Incorporating green objectives explicitly in institutional mandates can be useful, but that task typically requires legal modification, and most mandates appear broad enough to accommodate green strategies in the institutional mission.

For green financing, NDFIs should develop a detailed internal strategy to illustrate how they intend to support the implementation of the government's C&E objectives.[1] For C&E risk, the strategy should consider different risk assessment approaches, including, where relevant, forward-looking assessments such as scenario analysis and stress testing to build a solid understanding of how C&E physical and transition risks can translate into financial risks.

Furthermore, an approach to reduce projects' negative C&E impacts that could ultimately undermine those projects' financial performance should be considered (which often is part of NDFIs' environmental and social risk management [ESRM] systems; refer to the "C&E Financial Risk Management" section later in this chapter for further details) (IADB 2021). Actions should also include a strategy on capacity building that includes quantitative targets (for example, in relation to the amount or share of green assets in credit and investment portfolios, as well as the carbon footprint from Scope 1, 2, and 3 greenhouse gas [GHG] emissions),[2] clear milestones, and monitoring and evaluation indicators to ensure that practical actions are taken to address key priorities for managing C&E risks and opportunities. Strategies could consider explicit alignment with the agenda around the Paris Agreement (refer to box 4.1).

---

**BOX 4.1**

## Paris Alignment and net-zero transition plans

A growing number of FIs are committing to align their lending and investment decisions with the Paris Agreement or other climate goals. Several initiatives, such as the GFANZ and the Net-Zero Banking Alliance, have been established to help FIs transition toward net-zero. Major commercial banks and MDBs (including the World Bank) have also made commitments related to net-zero or the Paris Alignment.[a]

In addition, supervisors around the world (including in the United States, Japan, the European Union, and the United Kingdom) are exploring their role in guiding the development of FIs' transition plans. Evaluating and monitoring the risks arising from plan misalignment can feed into the supervisory review process and the assessment of transition risks.

As the momentum is growing, FIs' approaches to net-zero or the Paris Alignment are heterogeneous; no common definition exists for what it means to achieve either. However, both generally entail developing approaches to reduce GHG emissions in FIs' lending and investment portfolios to align with pathways to net-zero by the middle of this century (UNEP FI n.d.).[b] Paris Alignment may also include objectives related to adaptation and resilience. Even though these approaches are diverse, several common elements can apply to FIs' approaches for both (Coalition of Finance Ministers for Climate Action 2021; GFANZ 2022; World Resources Institute 2021):

- *Data collection* usually involves collecting data on portfolio-wide emissions to inform FIs' targets, transition plans, and client engagement. The Partnership for Carbon Accounting Financials (n.d.)[c] was developed to help FIs assess and disclose GHG emissions associated with financing activities.

- *Target-setting* usually involves setting quantitative emission reduction targets using global guidance such as the Science-Based Targets Initiative (n.d.).[d]

- *Steering* involves adjusting FIs' lending and investment portfolios in line with the agreed target. Several tools have been developed to support this process. For example, the Paris Agreement Capital Transition Assessment tool (Climate Scenario Analysis Program, n.d.) can be used to assess whether investment or lending portfolios are in line with a variety of climate scenarios.[e]

- *Tracking progress* usually involves developing a transition plan, which allows FIs to anticipate the transition and prepare for adjustments to their business models. The plan should include a detailed multiyear roadmap with clear targets and actions (Grantham Research Institute 2022). Initiatives such as the GFANZ and the Net-Zero Banking Alliance have been established to support this process. To ensure integrity and credibility, the transition plan should include (a) a definition of the current emission baseline (business-as-usual scenario); (b) commitment to reduce Scope 1, 2, or 3 emissions at entry; and (c) interim targets (as relevant). Ideally, institutional processes for quality assurance should also be set up and may involve ex ante validation of the transition plan, including baseline and targets. Reporting on and independent verification of progress during

*continued*

**Box 4.1,** *continued*

plan implementation and target achievement could be considered.

FIs aiming to align lending and investment portfolios with the Paris Agreement are confronted with many challenges, including the lack of a clear definition of Paris Alignment and net-zero, a lack of sufficient data to track and measure targets, and the wide range of methods being used to operationalize the concept and its commitments. Methods are also not easily comparable and can lead to different outcomes, allowing room for interpretation and, therefore, "greenwashing."

*Note:* FI = financial institution; GFANZ = Glasgow Financial Alliance for Net Zero; GHG = greenhouse gas; MDB = Multilateral Development Bank.

a. The World Bank has committed to align all its financing operations with the goals of the Paris Agreement in its Climate Change Action Plan 2021–25. The Paris Alignment of these new financing flows is the most comprehensive institutional undertaking ever done by the World Bank to reconcile development and climate. The World Bank is on track to align 100 percent of new operations, starting from July 1, 2023. For the Multilateral Investment Guarantee Agency, 85 percent of new operations will be aligned starting July 1, 2023, and 100 percent from July 1, 2025. This work is part of a broader MDB vision to align financing flows with the objectives of the Paris Agreement.

b. The Net-Zero Banking Alliance defines *net-zero/Paris Alignment* as the transition of all operational and attributable GHG emissions from lending and investment portfolios to align with pathways to net-zero by the middle of this century, or sooner, including carbon dioxide emissions reaching net-zero by 2050 at the latest, consistent with a maximum temperature rise of 1.5°C above preindustrial levels by 2100.

c. https://carbonaccountingfinancials.com/.

d. https://sciencebasedtargets.org/.

e. https://2degrees-investing.org/resource/pacta/

Moreover, NDFIs should consider their role in addressing greenwashing practices, providing an example to the financial sector, and should include support for the development of relevant standards and policies to reduce the potential for market actors to make unsubstantiated claims about the demonstrated environmental merits of their products and services. The strategy should be endorsed by NDFIs' boards of directors or senior management to ensure accountability. NDFIs could consider launching the internal strategy publicly to lead by example and demonstrate their commitment to the agenda.

Equally important is for NDFIs to develop the appropriate governance framework for delivering on the internal strategy. Well-informed decision-making and coordination at every level (including municipal and local levels) are important to ensure the effectiveness of greening NDFIs. For this reason, NDFIs should develop an appropriate internal governance framework to make informed decisions on how C&E risks and opportunities are managed. This work may involve, for example, ensuring that a board representative is responsible for monitoring and managing C&E risks and opportunities. Securing board support at an early stage is important to demonstrate commitment to and leadership for the agenda. Relevant committees and departments should also be identified to ensure role clarity and responsibilities for implementing the internal strategy. It may also involve establishing a specific department or a cross-functional working group to coordinate and implement C&E-related decisions and priorities. In some cases, it may be helpful to adjust the NDFIs' formal mandate to explicitly include elements related to C&E, although this is not a prerequisite for greening NDFIs' operations (refer to box 3.1 on good practices on governance and strategy).

NDFIs should leverage international and national networks to build the required expertise on green financing, C&E risk management, and disclosure and reporting. A wide range of initiatives are supporting the agenda to green NDFIs. As noted in the introduction, several guidance notes have already been developed, including by the Inter-American Development Bank, the United Nations Development Programme, and the International Development Finance Club. NDFIs could leverage these international resources and networks to develop capacity-building programs on key topics. At the same time, NDFIs should strengthen collaboration with public authorities to ensure that its internal strategy is fully aligned with a country's C&E objectives. Engagement with authorities may also be important to support specific policy agendas (for example, developing a project pipeline; see further details in the following section, "Green Financing Sources and Uses").

Concerns exist that focusing on C&E activities by NDFIs possibly can affect financing flows to other underserved segments, such as small businesses; however, such a focus can also present opportunities. Micro, small, and medium enterprises (MSMEs) account for a large share of firms and employment in many countries. Most MSMEs operate in the services industry in sectors with relatively low emissions, such as retail commerce, hospitality, repairs, and personal or enterprise services. However, MSMEs in the manufacturing sector that are integrated into value chains face growing pressure to green their operations, as analysis of the greenness of large firms turns its focus to Scope 3 emissions (that is, emissions through firms' value chain). Although MSME clients increasingly pay attention to firms' green credentials, MSMEs often need their cash flow for purposes other than green investments and are unsure how to start on their green journey. At the same time, MSMEs face challenges with access to credit due to lack of physical collateral, weaker balance sheets, and lack of credit history.

For those reasons and also for their socioeconomic importance, MSMEs are typically a priority sector for NDFIs. However, NDFIs' focus on green activities could further hamper MSMEs' access to credit. Requirements for NDFI borrowers to report their emissions or obtain green certifications can present challenges for MSMEs. However, NDFI green operations can also provide MSMEs with equity or loans in new green technologies that can enhance productivity and increase cash flows, as well as advisory services to green small businesses (refer to box 4.2). Development of financial solutions to fund investments that increase MSME adaptation to climate finance is an area of opportunity.

## GREEN FINANCING SOURCES AND USES

Pipeline development and project preparation for green projects are critical to ensure capital flows to priority sectors for C&E objectives. The lack of an adequate, bankable project pipeline is often cited as a key challenge to scaling up green financing—sometimes even more challenging than access to the financing itself. NDFIs have a role to play in identifying and developing bankable green projects.

First, building on their expertise, stakeholder connections, and understanding of the local context, NDFIs could provide technical assistance to support project preparation, especially in sectors in which green investment is needed the most. Second, market education could be provided to project developers and

## Examples of NDFI green MSME products

Nacional Financiera in Mexico has operated the Massive Business Eco-Credit Program for more than a decade. Through this program, Nacional Financiera offers a credit line to the Energy Savings Trust Fund, which in turn provides credits to the final beneficiaries. Financing is offered at preferential rates, and credit repayments are made through electricity billing. Electricity savings are used for loan repayment without affecting the firm's cash flow, while the involvement of the electricity company in the loan collection through the electricity billing reduces the MSME credit risk that traditionally impedes access to investment loans.

Banco do Brasil, a state-owned commercial bank with the mission to support sustainable economic development in Brazil, will begin offering sustainability-linked loans to companies committed to reducing their carbon footprint through their value chain under a recently approved World Bank project. The initiative also includes a US$98 million pilot Climate Debt Fund, which is expected to leverage private capital to expand sustainability-linked finance in the broader economy. Under the program, Banco do

Brasil will offer its clients packages that integrate financing with support to access carbon markets through a "one-stop shop." This program will provide Brazilian firms—small and midsize companies in particular—with an accessible, end-to-end service starting from measuring their carbon footprint to generating returns from high-integrity carbon credits.

Bpifrance Ecotechnologies provides equity and convertible loans to innovative MSMEs active in carbon-free renewable energies and green chemistry, as well as in the circular economy (waste recovery, ecodesign of products, and industrial ecology). They invest in tickets from €2 million to €10 million, systematically seeking co-investment with private players in the logic of a wise investor.

To help MSMEs begin their green transition, NDFIs can offer a variety of nonfinancial products. The Strategic Banking Corporation of Ireland offers MSMEs vouchers for green audits. Bpifrance offers a free information technology self-diagnosis, called "The Climatomètre," to help firms assess their climate maturity, as well as consulting services.

*Note:* MSME = micro, small, and medium enterprise; NDFI = National Development Financial Institution.

financiers to raise awareness of investment opportunities, for example, through sector studies or outreach programs. Third, NDFIs could simplify the process of developing projects through standardization. For example, this work may include standardizing project documents to minimize the need for extensive negotiations and providing a common set of service providers (such as technical and insurance advisers) to achieve bulk discounts and lower fees. It may also involve offering commercial co-financing on a programmatic basis to facilitate investment at scale. By standardizing processes at the country and program levels, these approaches enable competitive tendering, faster delivery, and lower prices. Finally, NDFIs could also mobilize private funds toward project preparation by co-investing with institutions such as the International Finance Corporation (IFC) and other green-oriented investors in project preparation facilities. Private investors participating in those facilities have the option to recover those costs by participating in a project's debt and equity financing.

Mobilizing private financing for green projects should be a primary objective for NDFIs; mandates and mission statements should incorporate references to crowding in private sector finance to meet C&E goals. Focusing on crowding in private sector finance promotes leverage and efficient use of NDFI resources and does not preclude them from providing credit directly to borrowers but encourages them to shift their focus toward co-financing and risk-sharing mechanisms (Gutierrez and Kliatskova 2021). Having a clear understanding of market barriers will allow NDFIs to develop innovative financing approaches tailored to the local context and to leverage their areas of expertise, as well as to manage the challenges (refer also to table 4.1). Beyond the private sector, NDFIs should also explore ways to engage with State-Owned Enterprises (SOEs), which are important players in both the climate mitigation and adaptation agenda. Box 4.3 provides further details on how NDFIs can facilitate SOEs' climate action.

**TABLE 4.1 Potential approaches to address barriers to stimulating green investments from the private sector**

| MARKET BARRIER | APPROACHES TO ADDRESS THE BARRIER |
|---|---|
| *Perceived high riskiness of green projects:* Significant real or perceived riskiness of green projects increases the cost of capital and prevents projects from moving forward. For example, offtake and credit risks can lead to high underwriting costs for clean energy and energy-efficiency projects. Construction risk, particularly for nascent technologies with a limited track record, can lead to a shortage of capital in the project development phase. | • *Co-investment, including subordination:* If a project can secure financing for only a portion of its costs, NDFIs can provide gap financing to help close the deal. These instruments can have different structures, terms, and tenors. Taking a subordinated position in the capital stack and providing first-loss capital structures can further mitigate the risks and effectively mobilize additional funding sources.<br>• *Credit enhancements, including guarantees, insurance, first-loss capital, and loan-loss reserves:* In addition to de-risking projects, credit enhancements can help investors gain experience in lesser-known sectors, build their internal capacity, and shape their risk perception (for example, refer to McKinsey and Co. 2016). Guarantees are flexible instruments that can be tailored to different circumstances and types of risk. Loan-loss reserve funds can be structured in different ways to have a similar crowding-in effect—for example, by providing first- or second-loss provisions to increase private sector risk sharing.<br>• *Capital market access:* NDFIs can help connect local and international capital markets with projects that are beyond the high-risk development phase. These operational projects can offer competitive risk-adjusted returns and may be more suitable to meet institutional investors' risk appetite. For EMDEs, access to local capital markets can help avoid the need for expensive currency hedging products. Increasing local investor participation can build confidence in the market and increase overall willingness to invest.<br>• *Equity investments:* NDFIs could consider expanding their equity investments to capture the upside potential of projects, which, in turn, could help finance other NDFI investments. Taking equity positions may increase the NDFI's influence on the company's transition pathway (ODI 2020). Equity investments could be done through public-private green equity funds, with NDFIs acting as anchor investors, mobilizing private funds toward green equity investments, and developing capital markets. |
| *High up-front financing costs, high transaction costs, and long payback periods:* Green projects (for example, renewable energy, energy efficiency) often require a significant up-front capital investment and have long maturity profiles. The transaction costs of these investments are also generally higher in EMDEs (for example, due to lack of institutional capacity or lack of a regulatory enabling environment). These factors could increase the cost for investors to identify, assess, and manage these projects. | • *Co-investment and loan syndication:* To alleviate the up-front capital requirement, NDFIs could co-invest with private investors, potentially taking a subordinate position, to provide further risk mitigation. Through loan syndication, NDFIs can add value by structuring deals and acting as facilitator between project developers and investors.<br>• *Credit enhancements, such as guarantees, insurance, and loan-loss reserves:* NDFIs can provide credit enhancements by offering longer maturities, differentiated pricing structure, or more favorable debt repayment schedules.<br>• *Refinancing:* NDFIs can provide refinancing to recycle more expensive capital during the high-risk construction stage to less expensive capital at the operational stage, when cash flows are steady. |

*continued*

**TABLE 4.1,** *continued*

| MARKET BARRIER | APPROACHES TO ADDRESS THE BARRIER |
|---|---|
| *Small ticket size and disaggregated projects:* Small and geographically dispersed projects (for example, residential or small business energy efficiency projects) are often not cost-effective for private lenders to underwrite. The high transaction cost creates barriers for small-scale projects to access financing. | • *Aggregation and warehousing:* NDFIs can aggregate small, dissimilar, and difficult-to-evaluate projects that are not cost-effective to underwrite on their own. NDFIs could underwrite and warehouse the loans directly, either keeping them as on-balance-sheet investments or aggregating as an intermediary for other investors. Pooling these loans diversifies risk and achieves scale, making them more attractive to investors.<br>• *Securitization:* By pooling projects or transforming illiquid assets into tradable securities, NDFIs can lower transaction costs and spread the risk, making projects more attractive for private or institutional investors. |
| *Limited C&E expertise and lack of ability to identify and classify projects:* Investors, lenders, or project developers are often unfamiliar with emerging low-carbon technologies and other green projects. Wholesale actors may be unaware of the opportunities in the green financing market, leading to a disconnect between capital supply and demand, as well as to underinvestment in green technologies. Local banks may lack the knowledge to adapt underwriting methods, as assessing the economic viability of green projects requires specific technical expertise. | • *Demonstration investment:* NDFIs can take on early-stage investments, which private investors often shy away from. By developing a track record and filling information gaps, NDFIs can build confidence in the market for new technologies.<br>• *Technical assistance:* Given NDFIs' proximity to the government and local markets, NDFIs are well placed to educate local financiers about the investment opportunities and risks in green sectors.<br>• *Green credit lines:* NDFIs can provide green credit lines to foster lending to green projects through local institutions. Through this process and additional technical assistance, NDFIs could increase local FIs' awareness and expertise in green credit products, thus expanding the local green-lending market. |
| *Limited consumer understanding:* Consumers may have difficulty perceiving the economic benefits of green projects (for example, energy efficiency and distributed small- and medium-scale renewable energy projects). This issue could reduce interest in taking on associated public or private support programs (for example, specialized lending programs for energy efficiency or home solar). | • *Market education:* NDFIs can provide training and support to consumers and end users to generate demand for public or private support programs (for example, specialized lending for home solar).<br>• *Customer solutions:* NDFIs can ensure that end users face minimal complexity when considering a clean-energy solution by developing accessible processes to connect lending programs to consumers. |
| *Regulatory and policy risk:* The lack of an enabling regulatory and policy environment is a key challenge for green investments in EMDEs. Sudden changes to policies and regulations can increase investment uncertainty and reduce private investors' appetite for green projects. | • *First-loss provisions and loan-loss reserves:* NDFIs can reserve capital to cover a certain portion of a project's losses. A reserve can be in the first-loss or second-loss position in relation to the lender. This structure assures a lender that some portion of potential losses would be covered or shared by the NDFI.<br>• *Coordination and technical assistance:* NDFIs can function as the bridge between local governments and the market and help drive regulatory reforms that further de-risk green projects and create a more stable, policy-enabling environment. |
| *Currency risk:* Local capital markets often lack the depth to supply the financing needed for green investments, meaning that many projects must rely on foreign investment support. Owing to macroeconomic instability and other factors, EMDEs are often vulnerable to currency fluctuations. The depreciation of local currencies could increase the risk for foreign investors, particularly for capital-intensive projects with cash flows in local currencies. Conversely, investments denominated in the euro or dollar can create risk for local borrowers to service their debt obligations. | • *Currency hedge:* The costs of hedging products can be high, especially for countries with a history of unstable exchange rates and high political instability. NDFIs can build on existing models to create cost-effective local hedging facilities, which, in turn, could enable more foreign investment in low-carbon projects.[a] |

*continued*

**TABLE 4.1,** *continued*

| MARKET BARRIER | APPROACHES TO ADDRESS THE BARRIER |
|---|---|
| *Offtake risk:* The creditworthiness of (often state-owned) utilities in EMDEs is highly unstable. Utilities may fail to meet their obligations under power-purchase agreements (that is, purchase the power at the agreed-on price), which puts the return for investors and project developers at risk. Debt investors in many countries will price this risk into their required returns, which reduces the amount of debt that projects can attract. It can also lead to an increase in energy prices that are eventually charged to consumers. | • *Co-investment through subordination:* By providing subordinated financing, NDFIs can effectively provide a buffer for senior private capital, boosting the attractiveness of the project.<br>• *Credit enhancements, such as guarantees, insurance, and loan-loss reserves:* Credit enhancements can be designed to backstop power purchase agreements. This design can facilitate utility lending in EMDEs and assure lenders that losses will be shared. |

*Source:* Table original to this publication.
*Note:* C&E = climate and environmental; EMDE = emerging markets and developing economies; FI = financial institution; NDFI = National Development Financial Institution.
a. For example, the Currency Exchange Fund (TCX) or Indian Currency Hedging Facility.

---

**BOX 4.3**

## Facilitating climate action by SOEs

SOEs are critical players in the climate agenda. On the one hand, SOEs are a major source of GHG emissions, reflecting some of the main sectors in which they operate, such as electricity generation or utilities. SOEs account for at least 7.49 gigatons of carbon dioxide equivalent ($GtCO_2e$) annually in direct (Scope 1) emissions,[a] which represented approximately 14 percent of total annual average global GHG emissions between 2010 and 2019.[b] On the other hand, SOEs also have a role to play in adaptation and resilience, because they account for over half of the infrastructure investment in LICs and MICs, including power, water, and transport, all of which have to increasingly adapt to the impacts of climate change (World Bank 2022).

NDFIs should provide targeted support to enable SOEs' low-carbon and climate-resilient transition. NDFIs are major financiers of SOEs; therefore, they are best placed to financially support SOEs' green investments and encourage sound C&E risk management in SOE projects through the application of relevant frameworks. Although some of the approaches suggested in table 4.1 to facilitate private sector climate action may be applicable to SOEs, typically lower SOE profitability (partly reflecting government mandates and policy objectives) could limit the effectiveness of marketwide policy interventions designed to engage with private companies. In addition, significant heterogeneity exists among SOEs (for example, level of capacity, mandates, and relationships with governments). NDFIs' approaches to facilitating SOE climate action can include the following, depending on SOE governance structure and mandates:

• Improving SOEs' access to financing for low-carbon, climate-resilient activities (for example, through concessional loans);

• Investments in supporting public infrastructure (for example, transmission lines, grid expansion);

• Providing capacity building to improve SOE climate risk assessments and climate disclosures; and

• Providing technical and financial support to improve SOEs' ability to attract private climate financing (for example, facilitate reforms to improve SOEs' creditworthiness or long-term financial stability and use of de-risking instruments such as guarantees) (Benoit, Clark, and Schwarz 2022; World Bank 2022).

*Note:* C&E = climate and environmental; GHG = greenhouse gas; LIC = low-income country; MIC = middle-income country; NDFIs = National Development Financial Institutions; SOE = state-owned enterprise.
a. Estimated GHG emission from SOEs is based on data from 300 major SOEs (Clark and Benoit 2022).
b. Total global GHG emissions averaged 54.4 $GtCO_2e$ between 2010 and 2019 (UNEP 2022).

NDFIs should also aim to expand their offerings in climate adaptation financing. Funding for climate adaptation and resilience objectives is challenging and may require mechanisms different from those for more mainstream green investments. Although NDFIs are important players in the adaptation space, the relative financing gap for most countries remains significant as compared with mitigation financing. NDFIs could contribute to building the business case for adaptation financing and to enhancing the understanding of private investors and other relevant stakeholders about the potential economic benefits. For example, through capacity-building and demonstration investments, NDFIs could show the benefits of financing investments in sectors requiring adaptation financing, such as climate-resilient agricultural practices or infrastructure (refer to box 4.4).

Similarly, NDFIs can promote greater investment in biodiversity, the conservation and restoration of ecosystem services, and nature-based finance. Given the importance of nature and ecosystem services for sustainable development, it is imperative for NDFIs to consider protecting and preserving these services as part of their activities (for example, refer to IDFC 2022; WWF and The Biodiversity Consultancy 2021).

NDFIs are well placed to take a more active role in scaling up biodiversity and nature-positive investments by focusing on investing in projects that enhance or restore biodiversity, as well as on incorporating nature-based solutions in their portfolios and strategic decision-making to reduce harm to biodiversity. The economic benefits of nature-related finance may be significant; however, awareness of these types of investments is generally low. This lack of awareness provides NDFIs with an important market education role, as well as an incentive to mainstream biodiversity and nature-based solutions in their portfolios and investment decision-making processes. NDFIs have several tools that could provide support by identifying biodiversity-related risks and opportunities.[3] Moreover, NDFIs could provide support to governments to create strategic, technical, and legal frameworks favorable to biodiversity.

Finally, NDFIs could increase the private sector's participation in green financing markets and carbon markets by acting as a first mover and providing capacity building. In many countries, NDFIs have often acted as the first mover to issue green bonds, which not only is an effective way to raise capital to finance green projects, but also can raise the profile of green bonds with other potential issuers, thus providing an opportunity to deepen the local green bond market. NDFIs can take similar actions to stimulate interest in other novel markets, including carbon markets and sustainability-linked instruments, which can be a source for results-based funding for NDFIs (refer to box 4.5 for further details on NDFIs' potential role in carbon markets).

Beyond stimulating green financing instruments and carbon markets, NDFIs could also increase the private sector's familiarity with C&E policy instruments, through technical assistance and piloting activities. For example, in the Republic of Korea, Korea Development Bank is responsible for piloting the application of the Korean Green Taxonomy (refer to appendix B).

NDFIs should aim to enhance their access to financing from international climate funds. Access on concessional terms can be valuable for several reasons. For example, concessional financing or grants may be required to support a project's preparation to increase its commercial viability. Concessional finance may also be required for urgent interventions that cannot be delayed without increasing transition costs. In countries transitioning away from fossil fuels, additional concessional financing is needed for plant retirements and transition.

BOX 4.4

## NDFIs' role in scaling up finance for adaptation and resilience

It is difficult to quantify current levels of adaptation and resilience investments from the private sector because these interventions are often part of larger investment and business activities. In comparison with mitigation projects, adaptation and resilience investments are also harder to define because they can take many forms. What constitutes "adaptation and resilience" depends largely on a country's circumstances. Despite these data limitations, estimates suggest that current levels of adaptation financing fall far short of needs. According to the Climate Policy Initiative, adaptation finance accounted for only 7.5 percent of climate finance in 2019–20, and the majority of tracked adaptation finance came from the public sector (CPI 2022). At the same time, estimates suggest that the economic benefits of investing in adaptation can far outweigh the costs.[a]

Adaptation and resilience investments from the private sector are lagging for several reasons. For instance, adaptation benefits tend to be difficult to monetize, have high transaction costs, and generally involve local public goods. Furthermore, low-income communities, which are most in need of these types of investments, tend to have low access to capital (World Bank 2022). Using NDFIs' resources to address these challenges could be key to unlocking private investments and could generate important development benefits for EMDEs. The following examples demonstrate how NDFIs could scale up adaptation and resilience investments:[b]

- *Support the government in long-term adaptation investment planning, building on priorities laid out in a country's National Adaptation Plan and NDC.* This support will help identify priority investments required to meet a country's adaptation and resilience needs. The investment plan should also involve market assessments to identify which projects are—or could become—commercially viable and which projects do not meet private sector investment criteria, even when below-market financing and de-risking are offered by NDFIs.
- *Support the preparation of "bankable" adaptation projects.* Once bankable projects have been identified, targeted support could be provided for project preparation and to help these projects enter the market. For example, this support may involve conducting feasibility studies to assess a project's risk and return, mapping cash flows, and identifying potential funding gaps or where NDFI risk mitigation may be required. It may also involve project structuring and coordinating project financing with relevant investors to close the transaction.
- *Strengthen financial incentives for private participation.* NDFIs could offer blended finance, credit enhancement, or other targeted measures to stimulate private investments in adaptation. These should, however, be designed on a case-by-case basis to address the specific financing challenges of different adaptation and resilience projects.
- *Encourage the use of innovative financing mechanisms.* Capacity building and technical assistance could be provided to help investors and project developers leverage new financing instruments for adaptation and resilience.[c]

*Note:* EMDEs = emerging markets and developing economies; NDC = Nationally Determined Contribution; NDFI = National Development Financial Institution.
a. For example, the Global Commission on Adaptation estimated that investing US$1.8 trillion globally in five target areas from 2020 to 2030 could produce US$7.1 trillion in total benefits, and spending US$800 million on early-warning systems in developing countries could reduce climate-related disaster losses by US$3 billion to US$16 billion per year.
b. The examples build on the recommendations from World Bank (2021a).
c. Several examples are offered by the International Institute for Sustainable Development (IISD 2023).

Access to international climate financing is especially important for smaller NDFIs, particularly those operating in low-income countries with shallow capital markets and fiscally constrained governments. Given their unique position as a bridge among international climate financing, the government, and local markets, NDFIs are well placed to act as an intermediary for blended financing to

## Opportunities for NDFIs to leverage carbon markets to enable private investments

Carbon markets are growing as many countries and corporations intend to use carbon credits toward their climate pledges. Some estimates suggest that carbon markets under the Paris Agreement could grow to US$300 billion per year by 2030 and up to US$1 trillion per year by 2050 (IETA and University of Maryland 2021).

NDFIs could play an important role in stimulating the demand and supply of carbon credits. The World Bank is deepening its engagement with NDFIs to stimulate carbon markets. For example, to stimulate demand, the World Bank is supporting NDFIs and other state-owned FIs in the design of financial instruments that leverage carbon markets to raise additional investments and enhance the return profile for green financing instruments. This work may involve combining carbon credits with other financial instruments, such as grants, labeled bonds, concessional loans, or guarantees to address key barriers associated with climate investments (Srinivasan et al. 2023).

To stimulate the supply of carbon credits, NDFIs may provide technical assistance to help participating firms adopt credible transition plans and targets, as well as to develop solutions to generate carbon credits. For example, this work may involve setting up institutional processes for validating and verifying the quality of transition plans and targets. It may also involve setting guidance and processes to assess the quality and integrity of carbon credits generated by participating firms.

Although carbon markets could enable investments and enhance the viability of climate action, carbon credit trading also faces challenges that are partly due to the fact that they take place within a highly heterogeneous and fragmented global market. Today, numerous carbon credit markets, registries, and exchange platforms coexist globally, each with its own specifications and quality standards, making it difficult for companies to select options to monetize their carbon credits. The fragmentation in carbon credit trading rules and institutions leads to wide price dispersion, adding uncertainty to the price outlook for carbon credit sellers.

*Note:* FI = financial institution; NDFI = National Development Financial Institution.

aggregate and optimize the use of different sources of capital (for example, concessional, nonconcessional, and private equity) to maximize the efficiency and impact of all capital available for green investments.

Despite these potential benefits, accessing international climate funds could be resource-intensive and complex. For example, strict requirements may exist for social and environmental safeguards, with which NDFIs must comply to access these climate funds. To address these challenges, governments and international partners could provide technical support to help NDFIs comply with international climate funding requirements.

## C&E FINANCIAL RISK MANAGEMENT

NDFIs should introduce holistic, although proportionate, approaches to address C&E financial risks, drawing on guidance from global principles. A better and more systemic understanding of C&E financial risks is an important first step to informing C&E risk management practices. NDFIs should adopt comprehensive C&E risk management approaches that consider risks from both the financial risk angle (that is, the financial risks that C&E factors pose to their portfolios and balance sheets) as well as the impact angle (that is, covering potential risks generated by their investment and lending practices and assessments at the loan origination level [often considered as part of ESRM; also refer to the "C&E Financial Risk Management" section in chapter 3 for a discussion of the two approaches]). Recognizing the nascency of C&E risk management practices for many NDFIs, the following discussion prioritizes a selection of critical steps to enhance current practices related to the consideration of financial risks.

Risk management frameworks can address the impacts and effects of C&E considerations on project performance as well as on the financial performance of institutional portfolios. Many NDFIs have already implemented systems to administer C&E risks at the project level as part of their ESRM systems. In addition, access to multilateral funds requires application of project safeguard frameworks as defined by the multilateral community (for example, World Bank safeguards [World Bank 2017], performance standards [IFC 2012]). These can focus on mitigating the negative impacts of a C&E project, which, in turn, could affect that project's financial performance. Institutions increasingly are applying more comprehensive frameworks that consider C&E risks and opportunities regardless of funding source. Adopting frameworks to address the impacts of C&E financial risks on an institution's balance sheet and portfolio is an emerging practice.

Global standards can support NDFIs' adoption of international good practices for addressing C&E financial risks. Notably, the Basel Committee on Banking Supervision Principles for Effective Management and Supervision of Climate-Related Financial Risks (BCBS 2022) has set expectations for banks and supervisors. These principles describe expectations about how banks should cover climate risks in governance and strategy, the internal control framework across different lines of defense (credit origination, risk function, and internal audit), the risk management process, capital and liquidity adequacy, reporting, and scenario analysis. In many cases, these principles also can apply to NDFIs, proportionate to the nature, scale, and complexity of their operations and the overall level of risk to which they are exposed and are willing to take.

Existing risk management frameworks can help NDFIs integrate C&E risks into credit or operational risk processes (IADB 2021), as well as into long-term strategies, governance arrangements, and the risk management frameworks themselves. NDFIs must assess and estimate the impact of C&E physical and transition risks on their investment and credit portfolios over the short, medium, and long term. NDFIs should consider appropriate mitigation mechanisms, including potential investment limits on exposed sectors.

Forward-looking assessments, such as scenario analysis and stress testing, can help NDFIs better understand the impact of C&E financial risks on their credit and investment portfolios. A simplified approach may involve assessing exposure to sectors or regions vulnerable to physical and transition risks by obtaining data on the sectoral and regional distribution of assets. A more advanced approach may involve a climate scenario analysis or stress test.[4] In such tests, a variety of climate, economic, and financial models are combined to estimate the impact of climate scenarios on losses and capital. The scope and granularity of stress tests depend on available data and models. Climate risk assessments and stress tests can help identify material risks and provide insights into various risk channels. Regulators and supervisors may request using the outcomes of such exercises over time, including in internal capital and liquidity adequacy assessments. In financial sectors less advanced in managing C&E risks, NDFIs could act as a first mover by implementing forward-looking C&E risk assessments to demonstrate the feasibility and value of such assessments to other private sector financial institutions. Such assessments could also increase local FIs' awareness of the impact of local C&E risk hot spots (for example, high-carbon sectors or flood-prone areas) on portfolios. Detailed and cutting-edge examples of how to conduct a climate analysis can be drawn from national regulators (for example, the European Central Bank and Financiera de Desarrollo Nacional in Colombia), global entities (such as the Financial Stability Board and the Network for Greening the Financial System, which also provides scenario inputs) and work done by multilaterals such as the World Bank and the International Monetary Fund (for example, refer to ECB 2022; IMF and World Bank 2022; and World Bank 2021b).

These efforts could be supported by harmonizing and obtaining relevant data needed for C&E risk assessments. NDFIs should ensure that their data aggregation capabilities and internal reporting frameworks can monitor material C&E-related financial risks. NDFIs should enhance the availability and quality of data needed to improve risk assessments. For example, NDFIs could consider collecting more granular data on clients' GHG emissions (including data from listed and nonlisted companies) and geospatial data on clients' operations (for example, location of main production facilities). Information from locally available natural-catastrophe models could also improve the physical risk scenario generation.

NDFIs should further develop their internal capacity to assess and manage C&E risks effectively. It will be important for NDFIs to adopt a dynamic approach and be flexible to adopt new and rapidly evolving practices. C&E risk assessments should be updated regularly because data availability and methodologies are rapidly evolving. One critical challenge identified by NDFIs (see the "C&E Financial Risk Management" section in chapter 3) is the need for more expertise with and understanding of C&E risks. To address this gap, tailored capacity-building programs, which could potentially leverage support from Multilateral Development Banks or other international partners, could be provided to build internal knowledge.

Evidence suggests that NDFIs may also be significantly exposed to nature-related risks, which requires enhanced risk management. The Finance for Biodiversity Initiative estimates NDFIs' "dependency risk" (that is, the share of activities that depend on nature and ecosystem services) to be approximately 40 percent of their total assets. In addition, the "nature at risk" from lending activities is estimated at US$800 billion annually, which is based on the value of the potential damage to nature resulting from deforestation and water use if investments are carried out without effective safeguards to mitigate such harm.[5] Moreover, many NDFIs do not apply biodiversity safeguards in investment decisions, relying instead on national environmental impact assessments that often fall short of international best practices in biodiversity risk management.

More work may be needed for NDFIs to understand, measure, and manage the nature-related risks in their portfolios, including their impacts and dependencies on nature. Scaling up finance in nature-based solutions and mainstreaming biodiversity considerations across strategies, analysis, and operations will help reduce dependencies and mitigate these risks.

## C&E DISCLOSURES AND REPORTING

NDFIs should enhance their C&E disclosure and reporting practices, which are important means to facilitate communication with clients, beneficiaries, and other stakeholders. Building on the Task Force on Climate-Related Financial Disclosures (TCFD) recommendations, NDFIs should work toward publishing meaningful disclosures on the implications of C&E risks and opportunities for their operations, aimed at providing decision-useful, forward-looking information that can be included in mainstream financial filings. In particular, NDFIs should disclose the key C&E risks to which they are exposed; the organization's governance around C&E risks and opportunities; the actual and potential impacts of C&E risks and opportunities on its activities, business model, and (long-term) strategy; and how the NDFI identifies, assesses, and manages C&E risks, including the metrics and targets it uses. Disclosure frameworks should embed the concept of complete materiality (or double materiality), covering the financial impact of climate-related risks on the one hand and the impact of banks' activities on both climate and social factors (inside-out perspective) on the other.

Furthermore, given the importance of nature-related and biodiversity risks and finance for NDFIs, they are also encouraged to engage with the Taskforce on Nature-Related Financial Disclosures (TNFD). The TNFD follows a structure similar to that of the TCFD and can help NDFIs incorporate nature-related risks and opportunities into their risk management and strategic planning processes. Moreover, NDFIs should familiarize themselves with impending global sustainability disclosure standards from the International Sustainability Standards Board (ISSB), which was set up under the International Financial Reporting Standards. The ISSB published its global sustainability standards in 2023, which have implications for NDFIs' reporting over time.

NDFIs should aim to improve the quality, transparency, and consistency of green financing–tracking methodologies, including methodologies that track the amount of private financing mobilized. As noted in the "Green Financing Sources and Uses" section in chapter 3, NDFIs follow different climate finance–tracking methodologies, which makes it difficult to track their climate financing. NDFIs should build internal capacity and introduce formal processes to track their green financing volumes, which can help assess their progress in achieving their C&E objectives, and to report this information both internally and externally.

To assess the effectiveness of their green financing, NDFIs can work together to harmonize climate finance–accounting methodologies, including those designed to track the amount of private financing mobilized. Methodologies for tracking climate financing should be aligned with global good practices and national green taxonomies where relevant.

## NOTES

1. In this context, policy and regulatory predictability are key because NDFIs need clarity about what sectors and technologies are being prioritized to reach countries' Nationally Determined Contribution (per the Paris Agreement) and other C&E goals.
2. *Scope 1* covers emissions from sources that an organization owns or controls directly. *Scope 2* are emissions that a company causes indirectly when the energy it purchases and uses is produced. *Scope 3* encompasses emissions that are not produced by the company

itself and are not the result of activities from assets owned or controlled by them but rather are by those for which it is indirectly responsible, up and down its value chain.

3. These tools include the Integrated Biodiversity Assessment Tool; footprinting through the Biodiversity Footprint Financial Institutions tool; the Global Biodiversity Score; or the Exploring Natural Capital Opportunities, Risks and Exposure tool.

4. A climate stress test is a forward-looking financial risk assessment consisting of several steps: (a) the identification of severe but plausible extreme weather scenarios that are tailored to the country context, (b) an assessment of expected economic direct and indirect impacts by using catastrophe models and adapted macroeconomic modeling frameworks, and (c) an assessment of financial impacts using financial stress test modeling to translate economic and financial impacts into financial soundness indicators (for example, capital adequacy ratio, probability of default).

5. Finance for Biodiversity Initiative (2021). Note that the Finance for Biodiversity Initiative uses the definition of Public Development Banks, which is slightly narrower than NDFIs.

## BIBLIOGRAPHY

BCBS (Basel Committee on Banking Supervision). 2022. *Principles for Effective Management and Supervision of Climate-Related Financial Risks*. Basel, Switzerland: BCBS.

Benoit, P., A. Clark, and M. Schwarz. 2022. "Decarbonization in State-Owned Companies: Lessons from a Comparative Analysis." *Journal of Cleaner Production* 355: 131796. https://doi.org/10.1016/j.jclepro.2022.131796.

Clark, A., and P. Benoit. 2022. *Greenhouse Gas Emissions from State-Owned Enterprises: A Preliminary Inventory*. New York: Columbia University.

Climate Scenario Analysis Program. n.d. https://2degrees-investing.org/resource/pacta/.

Coalition of Finance Ministers for Climate Action. 2021. *Introduction to Commitments and Measurement Methods for Private Financial Sector Portfolio Alignment with the Paris Agreement*. Washington, DC: Coalition of Finance Ministers for Climate Action.

CPI (Climate Policy Initiative). 2022. *Global Landscape of Climate Finance: A Decade of Data*. San Francisco, CA: CPI.

ECB (European Central Bank). 2022. *Climate Risk Stress Test*. Frankfurt, Germany: ECB.

Finance for Biodiversity Initiative. 2021. *Aligning Development Finance with Nature's Needs Estimating the Nature-Related Risks of Development Bank Investments*. https://www.naturefinance.net/wp-content/uploads/2022/09/Estimating-the-nature-related-risks-of-development-bank-investments.pdf.

GFANZ (Glasgow Financial Alliance for Net Zero). 2022. *Net-Zero Transition Planning*. New York: GFANZ.

Grantham Research Institute on Climate Change and the Environment. 2022. *Net Zero Transition Plans: A Supervisory Playbook for Prudential Authorities*. London, UK: London School of Economics and Political Science.

Gutierrez, E., and T. Kliatskova. 2021. *National Development FIs: Trends, Crisis Response Activities, and Lessons Learned*. Washington, DC: World Bank.

IADB (Inter-American Development Bank). 2021. *A Guidebook for National Development Banks on Climate Risks*. Washington, DC: IADB.

IDFC (International Development Finance Club). 2022. *Toolbox on Integrating Biodiversity into Strategies and Operations of Development Finance Institutions*. https://www.idfc.org/wp-content/uploads/2022/06/idfc-toolbox-biodiversity.pdf.

IETA (International Emissions Trading Association) and University of Maryland. 2021. *The Potential Role of Article 6 Compatible Carbon Markets in Reaching Net-Zero*. https://k5x2e9z8.rocketcdn.me/wp-content/uploads/2023/09/IETA_WorkingPaper_ThePotentialRoleofA6CompatibleCarbonMarketsinReachingNetZero_2021.pdf.

IFC (International Finance Corporation). 2012. "Policy on Environmental and Social Sustainability." IFC, Washington, DC. https://www.ifc.org/content/dam/ifc/doc/mgrt/sp-english-2012.pdf.

IISD (International Institute for Sustainable Development). 2023. *Innovative Financial Instruments for Climate Adaptation.* Winnipeg, Canada: IISD.

IMF (International Monetary Fund). 2022. *Financial Stability Report.* Washington, DC: IMF.

IMF (International Monetary Fund) and World Bank. 2022. *Bank Stress Testing of Physical Risks under Climate Change Macro Scenarios: Typhoon Risks to the Philippines.* Washington, DC: IMF.

McKinsey and Co. 2016. *Financing Change: How to Mobilize Private Sector Financing for Sustainable Infrastructure.* http://newclimateeconomy.report/2015/wp-content/uploads/sites/3/2016/01/Financing_change_How_to_mobilize_private-sector_financing_for_sustainable-_infrastructure.pdf.

ODI (Overseas Development Institute). 2020. *Securing Climate Finance through National Development Banks.* London: ODI.

Srinivasan et al. 2023. *Leveraging Carbon Markets to Enable Private Investment.* OMFIF Sustainable Policy Institute Blog. https://www.omfif.org/spijournal_winter_23_world-bank/.

UNEP (United Nations Environment Programme). 2022. *Emissions Gap Report 2022: The Closing Window—Climate Crisis Calls for Rapid Transformation of Societies.* Nairobi, Kenya: UNEP.

UNEP FI (United Nations Environment Programme–Finance Initiative). n.d. *Net-Zero Banking Alliance.* https://www.unepfi.org/net-zero-banking/.

World Bank. 2017. "World Bank Environmental and Social Framework." World Bank, Washington, DC. https://thedocs.worldbank.org/en/doc/837721522762050108-0290022018/original /ESFFramework.pdf.

World Bank. 2021a. *Enabling Private Investments in Climate Adaptation and Resilience.* Washington, DC: World Bank.

World Bank. 2021b. *Not-So-Magical Realism: A Climate Stress Test of the Colombian Banking System.* Washington, DC: World Bank.

World Bank. 2021c. *World Bank Group Climate Action Plan 2021–2025: Supporting Green, Resilient, and Inclusive Development.* Washington, DC: World Bank. https://www.worldbank.org/en/publication/paris-alignment.

World Bank. 2022. *Achieving Climate and Development Goals: The Financing Question.* Washington, DC: World Bank.

World Resources Institute. 2021. *How Banks Can Accelerate Net-Zero Emissions Commitments.* Washington, DC: World Resources Institute. https://www.wri.org/insights/banks-paris-alignment-net-zero-finance.

WWF and The Biodiversity Consultancy. 2021. *Public Development Banks and Biodiversity: How PDBs Can Align with the Post-2020 Global Biodiversity Framework.* Paris: WWF France.

# 5 Conclusions and Key Recommendations

## BACKGROUND

National Development Financial Institutions (NDFIs) play a key role in the provision of green financing by mobilizing private capital and fostering the development of green financing markets. NDFIs are the main providers of green financing in low-income and middle-income countries (LICs and MICs), reflecting their capacity to provide long-term funding and support for riskier projects. Furthermore, NDFIs can catalyze private sector financing through risk-sharing mechanisms such as co-financing instruments, credit enhancements, or partial credit guarantees. In numerous cases, NDFIs have piloted innovative green financing products—for example, green bonds (Nacional Financiera in Mexico) and sustainability-linked loans (Brazilian Development Bank in Brazil).

In the development of green products, NDFIs can help standardize contracts and set product standards and specifications. NDFIs can build capacity at different stages of the project cycle and, in many cases, can provide technical assistance to clients to green their operations. They can also lead by example in the development of taxonomies (for example, the Fideicomisos Instituidos en Relación con la Agricultura [FIRA] in Mexico has developed a taxonomy for agricultural activities), climate disclosures, and climate and environmental (C&E) risk management, as well as share the lessons learned from these practices with private financial institutions.

## CURRENT STATUS OF GREEN OBJECTIVES

Results from a World Bank survey indicate that most NDFIs have adopted green objectives and have incorporated C&E considerations into their operations, although the operationalization of those objectives can be strengthened. Most NDFIs surveyed have adopted green objectives, within their existing legal mandates; however, few have set concrete targets in relation to the Paris Agreement's Nationally Determined Contributions (NDCs) objectives. Most institutions have green financing targets and exclusions for nongreen activities.

Only one-third of NDFIs surveyed have created high-level committees, sustainability directorates, or special units focused on C&E aspects. Only about half reported their share of green assets, and the average is low, at 14 percent of the credit portfolio, primarily for mitigation projects. The use of green debt instruments and green fund accreditations is not generalized. Few institutions track private sector funding mobilized for green purposes.

## FACTORS IMPEDING SCALING UP GREEN FINANCING

NDFIs have identified several factors impeding the scaling up of green financing activities. The main obstacles include inadequate climate policies, funding gaps, lack of capacity and awareness of C&E issues both in the financial and real sectors, and the cost and complexities of green projects.

## WORKING TOWARD GREEN OBJECTIVES

NDFIs can take a range of actions in four broad categories to mobilize financing toward green objectives and manage C&E-related financial risks (refer to table 5.1):

1. Developing the green governance and strategic framework,

2. Scaling up financing to meet C&E objectives,

3. Assessing and managing C&E risks, and

4. Enhancing climate-related disclosures and reporting.

Actions to green NDFIs should be supported by an enabling policy environment. Establishing ambitious national C&E targets (for example, under the NDC) and developing legislation and plans to signal the government's long-term commitment to the green agenda are important. Policies such as carbon pricing, sectoral regulations and aligning broader fiscal and economic policies (for example, removing distortive fossil fuel subsidies to improve the commercial case for green projects) can further support a policy environment conducive to green NDFIs. Developing a national green taxonomy can help to ensure a common understanding of what economic activities can be considered as being aligned with C&E objectives. For financial sector authorities, it is equally important to develop the supervisory and regulatory reforms to facilitate the management of C&E risks and to develop policy actions to deepen green financing markets.[1]

Governments and financial regulators can also support NDFIs to close the funding gap, particularly in LICs and MICs. Governments could increase the provision of guarantees to facilitate NDFI access to multilateral funding and international capital markets for priority green projects, if debt sustainability considerations permit. Governments and financial regulators can also implement policies to foster capital market development and long-term finance, providing NDFIs with more options to leverage their own capital with long-term funding.

As they scale up operations to meet green financing needs, NDFIs must enhance their efficiency and ensure effective management and proper supervision. Regardless of their mandates, NDFIs should focus on complementing the private sector and crowding in private investors to provide financial solutions to

**TABLE 5.1 Overview of key policy toolkits to green NDFIs**

| CATEGORY | TOOLKIT | OBJECTIVE | EXPECTED OUTCOME |
|---|---|---|---|
| **Developing the green governance and strategic framework** | Develop an internal strategy, including quantitative and qualitative targets, clear milestones, and action plans, to address key C&E risks and opportunities and mobilize private sector funding for green projects. | Identify short-, medium-, and long-term priorities to manage C&E risks and mobilize green financing. | Align operations and incentives with the country's C&E goals, including NDC and long-term strategy. |
| | Develop an internal governance framework to deliver on commitments laid out in the internal strategy, including making board-level commitments, assigning individual responsibilities, and integrating C&E risks and opportunities into the institution's policies and risk appetite statement. | Ensure long-term commitment to the agenda, and define roles and responsibilities to ensure that the objectives in the internal strategy will be met. | |
| **Scaling up financing to meet C&E objectives** | Support the development of a pipeline of bankable projects, including providing technical assistance, raising awareness, and standardizing approaches and project preparation facilities. | Enhance the availability of green projects that meet private investors' risk and return preferences. | Improve risk-adjusted returns of green investments, and catalyze new markets for green growth. |
| | Develop innovative approaches to address market barriers for private sector green investments. | Stimulate private sector financing for climate action. | |
| | Improve access to concessional funds and grants through international climate funds (for example, GCF). | Ensure availability of funds to support climate investments. | |
| | Deepen green financing markets and carbon markets by actively participating in them or conducting capacity building and piloting. | Ensure the availability of funds to support climate investments, and raise the profile of green financing markets. | |
| **Assessing and managing C&E risks** | Adopt risk management frameworks that consider C&E risks and opportunities comprehensively. Conduct forward-looking assessments to understand how C&E risks translate into financial risks. | Enhance the awareness and understanding of future C&E risks under different scenarios. | Enhance the awareness and understanding of C&E risks. |
| | Improve data aggregation capabilities and internal reporting frameworks to harmonize and obtain relevant data for C&E risk assessments. | Improve the granularity and robustness of C&E risk assessments. | |
| | Build internal capacity to effectively assess and manage C&E risks. | Ensure C&E risks are monitored regularly over time. | |
| | Integrate C&E risks into existing risk management frameworks. | Ensure adequate measures are in place to manage the key C&E financial risks that have been identified through risk assessments. | |
| **Enhancing climate-related disclosures and reporting** | Implement climate-financing tracking methodologies, including those for private financing mobilized through NDFI investments. | Improve the quality, transparency, and consistency of climate finance data. | Improve transparency, and avoid greenwashing. |
| | Enhance disclosure of and reporting on C&E risks. | Enhance market transparency and the understanding of C&E risks and opportunities, in line with international standards, to guarantee comparable and consistent information. | |

*Source:* Table original to this publication.
*Note:* C&E = climate and environmental; GCF = Global Climate Fund; NDC = Nationally Determined Contribution; NDFI = National Development Financial Institution.

identified underserved segments or projects while preserving financial sustainability. A focus on servicing credit-constrained viable borrowers should be key to closing the financing gap and providing additionality to the private sector, while ensuring that private sector finance is not crowded out and net economic impact is maximized.

Although subsidized funding for green projects may be justified by large positive externalities, the focus on financial sustainability ensures that subsidized lending will not be the institution's primary focus, the potential for crowding out the private sector will be limited, the scope for corruption will be reduced, and innovation will be fostered. NDFIs should be effectively managed, and the incentives of management and staff should be aligned with institutional objectives through effective corporate governance, risk management, and mechanisms to evaluate institutional performance. Financial supervisory authorities should ensure that NDFIs are properly supervised and operate on a level playing field in relation to prudential regulations and competition.

In cases in which the environment does not support NDFI effectiveness, operating in a second tier through other financial intermediaries and raising funds in international capital markets may be advisable. Experience from FIRA in Mexico underlines the scope for second-tier institutions to become market referents for green financing.

To improve efficiency, governments could incentivize the greening of state-owned NDFIs by integrating C&E and private capital mobilization considerations into NDFIs' mandates or missions and aligning incentives throughout the institution through effective shareholding functions. Government agencies exerting the shareholding function on state-owned NDFIs could further incentivize C&E action by ensuring that mandates or strategies incorporate C&E and private capital mobilization objectives; by setting key performance indicators on green investments, NDC contributions, and capital market mobilization; and for green purposes to be reported to the shareholders and publicly disclosed. Linking remuneration policies and performance evaluation of management based on those indicators would further align incentives through the institution to develop green products and to embed C&E considerations in NDFIs' operations. These actions combined, while respecting the operational independence of the institutions, would prompt NDFIs to meet objectives by developing green financing products and incorporating C&E into their operations. In some instances, this course of action may require strengthening the way governments manage their NDFIs in line with Organisation for Economic Co-operation and Development guidelines on corporate governance of state-owned enterprises (OECD 2015).

## MDB SUPPORT FOR NDFIs

Based on the key priorities and challenges outlined in this report, the World Bank and other Multilateral Development Banks (MDBs) can provide targeted support to NDFIs. First, MDBs can provide funding support—including loans, investments, and guarantees in local currency denominations—to NDFIs seeking to green their operations and to pilot new green products. In addition, this assistance can include knowledge sharing and technical assistance for NDFIs to build their capacity in C&E risk management and green financing, including support to obtain climate funds accreditation, and to enhance the overall corporate governance in state-owned NDFIs, including support for government shareholding units. Furthermore, technical assistance is essential for the government and financial sector authorities to create an enabling environment for greening NDFIs, including supportive C&E policies, policies to support capital market development and green financing, and design and implementation of government programs to create awareness of C&E issues in the real sector and incentivize green investments. Finally, MDBs can monitor progress and share best practices on greening NDFI operations through data collection, research, and knowledge-sharing platforms.

## NOTE

1. For further guidance for financial-sector authorities, see World Bank (2021).

## BIBLIOGRAPHY

OECD (Organisation for Economic Co-operation and Development). 2015. *OECD Guidelines on Corporate Governance of State-Owned Enterprises.* Paris: OECD Publishing.

World Bank. 2021. *Toolkits for Policymakers to Green the Financial System.* Washington, DC: World Bank.

# Characteristics of NDFIs, from Survey Responses

## BACKGROUND

The World Bank launched a survey on greening National Development Financial Institutions (NDFIs) in January 2022 with the objective to explore their role in the green agenda. The survey included questions on the following:

- NDFIs' high-level commitments to the green agenda;
- Provision and tracking of green financing;
- Sources of funding, including access to green funding;
- Management of climate-related and environmental risks; and
- Challenges and aspirations for greening the NDFIs.

The detailed questions are provided in table A.1.

The survey was sent to 27 NDFIs that are the largest, as measured by their assets, or that are regional leaders in the climate and environmental agenda. The selection ensured coverage of different geographical regions and NDFIs' official mandates.

## SURVEY RESPONSES

Responses were received from 22 NDFIs, with wide geographical and income-level coverage. Of the 22 NDFIs, the distribution by income level is as follows: 3 are from high-income countries, 13 are from upper-middle-income countries, 4 are from lower-middle-income countries, and 2 are from low-income countries. Eight NDFIs are from Latin America, 4 are from Europe and Central Asia, 5 are from East Asia and Pacific, 3 are from Africa, and 2 are from South Asia. Nine do not have official mandates confined to a specific mission. Others have sector-specific mandates: 5 in agriculture; 3 in micro, small, and medium enterprises; 2 in local government; 2 in exports and foreign trade; and 1 in infrastructure (Xu et al. 2021). Together, the surveyed banks account for approximately 9 percent of global NDFI assets. A list of respondents is presented in table A.2.

## INTERPRETING THE RESULTS

When interpreting the survey's aggregate results, it is worth considering the drawbacks of the survey's design. The survey was sent to a preselected group of large NDFIs. The selection was based on the size of the development financial institution as well as to ensure wide geographic, income-level, and mandate coverage. In addition, NDFIs were selected based on their activities in pursuing a green agenda. Therefore, the results are not necessarily representative for the universe of NDFIs, as other NDFIs might be less active in the green financing space. Instead, these results can showcase the best practices of NDFIs in developing and pursuing a green agenda.

TABLE A.1 **"Greening NDFIs" questionnaire**

| MODULE | NO. | QUESTION | RESPONSE | DETAILS |
|---|---|---|---|---|
| **1. General information** | 1 | Name of your institution | | |
| | 2 | Does the mandate and/or mission of your institution include green, climate, or environmental objectives? | Yes/No | Please provide details. |
| | 3 | Has your institution developed a strategy to green its portfolio? | Yes/No | Please provide details. |
| | 4 | Has your institution made any public pledges or commitments to align its activities with international or national climate-related and environmental goals (for example, Paris Agreement, Nationally Determined Contributions [NDCs])? | Yes/No | Please provide details. |
| | 5 | Does your institution track green financing volumes across its activities? | Yes/No | Please provide details. |
| | 6 | Does your institution use a classification system to tag/identify green projects and activities? | Yes/No | Please provide details. |
| | 7 | Is your institution involved in the national climate financing process and the implementation of the country's NDCs or other broader climate/green financing policy discussions? | Yes/No | Please provide details. |
| **2. Green financing** | 8 | Does your institution have specific green financing targets? | Yes/No | Please provide details. |
| | 9 | Does your institution exclude financing for specific (nongreen) projects? | Yes/No | Please provide details. |
| | 10 | What are the share and absolute volumes of green assets in your credit and investment portfolios? If possible, please provide a breakdown of climate-related financing and financing for broader environmental objectives. Please provide an estimate if not available or not tracked. | | |
| | | Green assets in credit portfolio | Share (%) | |
| | | Green assets in credit portfolio | Total volume | |
| | | Green assets in investment portfolio | Share (%) | |
| | | Green assets in investment portfolio | Total volume | |
| | 11 | What is the absolute volume of financing for climate mitigation versus climate adaptation projects? What is the percentage of climate financing that goes toward mitigation versus toward adaptation? Please provide an estimate if not available or not tracked. | | |
| | | Total volume of climate mitigation financing | Total volume | |
| | | Percentage of climate financing that goes toward climate mitigation | Share (%) | |
| | | Total volume of climate adaptation financing | Total volume | |
| | | Percentage of climate financing that goes toward climate adaptation | Share (%) | |

**TABLE A.1**, *continued*

| MODULE | NO. | QUESTION | RESPONSE | DETAILS |
|---|---|---|---|---|
| | 12 | What are the main sectors that your institution is financing to meet its climate and environmental objectives? | Please select all that apply: <br>• Power <br>• Transport <br>• Building <br>• Industry <br>• Land use <br>• Agriculture <br>• Other, please specify: | |
| | 13 | Who are the main actors/clients to whom your institution is providing green financing? | | |
| | 14 | To the extent possible, please provide details on type of financing and financial instruments your institution employs for green financing objectives. | | |
| | 15 | Are you tracking the level of private financing that is mobilized by your financing activities? | Yes/No | Please provide details. |
| | 16 | Are you collaborating with subnational development banks to channel financing to the local level? | Yes/No | Please provide details. |
| | 17 | What are the (3–5) key challenges/barriers to scaling up financing for climate and environmental objectives? Please elaborate. | | |
| 3. Sources of funding and pricing | 18 | To what national sources of funding do you have access? | | |
| | 19 | To what international sources of finance do you have access? | | |
| | 20 | Does your institution have access to national and/or international capital markets? | Yes/No | Please provide details. |
| | 21 | Has your institution issued a green bond? | Yes/No | Please provide details. |
| | 22 | Has your institution issued a sustainability-linked bond? | Yes/No | Please provide details. |
| | 23 | Is your institution accredited by international climate funds (such as the Green Climate Fund)? | Yes/No | Please provide details. |
| | 24 | What proportion of your climate-related portfolio is subsidized (that is, priced at below cost of funding, administration, credit risk, and target return on capital)? | | |
| | 25 | If part of your climate-related portfolio is subsidized, what is the source of the subsidy (for example, budgetary subsidies, international climate funds, multilateral funding, or cross-subsidization from other portfolio activities)? | | |

*continued*

**TABLE A.1,** *continued*

| MODULE | NO. | QUESTION | RESPONSE | DETAILS |
|---|---|---|---|---|
| **4. Climate-related and environmental risk management** | 26 | Does your financial institution expect that climate-related and environmental financial risks will affect its business model (over the short, medium, and long term)? | Yes/No | If yes, please explain how and over what time frames. If no, please explain why not. |
| | 27 | Has your institution assessed the impact of climate-related and environmental financial risks on its portfolio (over the short, medium, and long term)? | Yes/No | Please provide details. |
| | 28 | Has your institution integrated the consideration of climate-related and environmental financial risk into its governance arrangements? | Yes/No | Please provide details. |
| | 29 | Is your (long-term) strategy incorporating climate-related and environmental financial risk considerations? | Yes/No | Please provide details. |
| | 30 | Is the consideration of climate-related and environmental financial risk embedded in your risk management frameworks? | Yes/No | Please provide details. |
| | 31 | Does your institution conduct scenario analysis or stress testing to assess climate-related and environmental financial risk? | Yes/No | Please provide details. |
| | 32 | Does your institution report on climate-related and environmental risk (for example, in line with the FSB Task Force on Climate-Related Financial Disclosures recommendations)? | Yes/No | Please provide details. |
| | 33 | Does your institution use any specific targets, tools, or metrics to assess climate-related and environmental financial risk? | Yes/No | Please provide details. |
| | 34 | What data are you using to inform your climate risk analysis? | | Please provide any specific data gaps you have identified. |
| | 35 | What are the (3–5) key challenges in identifying, assessing, monitoring, managing, and disclosing climate-related and environmental financial risk? Please elaborate. | | |
| | 36 | Does your institution have a system to administer and manage environmental risks created by its portfolio, including through the application of environmental safeguards? | | |
| **5. Other issues** | 37 | What are the main actions you plan to undertake for "greening" your institution in the next 1–5 years related to<br><br>(a) scaling up financing to meet climate and environmental objectives?<br><br>(b) identifying, assessing, monitoring, managing, and disclosing climate-related and environmental risks? | | |
| | 38 | Are there other relevant issues related to "greening" your institution that you would like to share? | | |
| **6. Contact information** | 39 | Name of the person(s) responsible for filling out the questionnaire | | |
| | | Position | | |
| | | Email | | |
| | | Telephone number | | |

*Source:* Table original to this publication.
*Note:* FSB = Financial Stability Board; NDC = Nationally Determined Contribution; NDFI = National Development Financial Institution.

**TABLE A.2 List of NDFIs surveyed**

| NO. | NDFI | COUNTRY OF HEADQUARTERS | INCOME LEVEL OF COUNTRY OF HEADQUARTERS | MANDATE |
|---|---|---|---|---|
| 1 | Banco de Inversión y Comercio Exterior | Argentina | UMIC | FLEX |
| 2 | Bangladesh Krishi Bank | Bangladesh | LMIC | AGRI |
| 3 | Brazilian Development Bank | Brazil | UMIC | FLEX |
| 4 | Financiera de Desarrollo Nacional | Colombia | UMIC | LOCAL |
| 5 | Corporación Financiera Nacional | Ecuador | UMIC | MSME |
| 6 | Kreditanstalt für Wiederaufbau | Germany | HIC | FLEX |
| 7 | National Bank for Agriculture and Rural Development | India | LMIC | AGRI |
| 8 | PT Sarana Multi Infrastruktur | Indonesia | LMIC | INFRA |
| 9 | Industrial Bank of Korea | Korea, Rep. | HIC | MSME |
| 10 | Korea Development Bank | Korea, Rep. | HIC | FLEX |
| 11 | Nacional Financiera | Mexico | UMIC | MSME |
| 12 | Fideicomisos Instituidos en Relación con la Agricultura | Mexico | UMIC | AGRI |
| 13 | Banco Nacional de Obras y Servicios Públicos | Mexico | UMIC | LOCAL |
| 14 | Banco Nacional de Comercio Exterior | Mexico | UMIC | EXIM |
| 15 | Landbank | Philippines | LMIC | AGRI |
| 16 | Development Bank of Rwanda | Rwanda | LIC | FLEX |
| 17 | Development Bank of Southern Africa | South Africa | UMIC | FLEX |
| 18 | Bank for Agriculture and Agricultural Cooperatives | Thailand | UMIC | AGRI |
| 19 | Export Credit Bank of Türkiye | Türkiye | UMIC | EXIM |
| 20 | Türkiye Sinai Kalkinma Bankasi | Türkiye | UMIC | FLEX |
| 21 | Türkiye Kalkinma ve Yatirim Bankasi | Türkiye | UMIC | FLEX |
| 22 | Uganda Development Bank | Uganda | LIC | FLEX |

*Source:* Table original to this publication. Data on mandate are from Xu et al. 2021.
*Note:* Flexible (FLEX) means that official mandates are not confined to a specific mission. If an NDFI's mandate is not flexible, the mandate is further classified according to its sectoral or client focus, including rural and agricultural development (AGRI), promoting exports and foreign trade (EXIM), infrastructure (INFRA), local government (LOCAL), and micro, small, and medium enterprises (MSMEs). HIC = high-income country; LIC = low-income country; LMIC = lower-middle-income country; NDFI = National Development Financial Institution; UMIC = upper-middle-income country (World Bank classifications).

## BIBLIOGRAPHY

Xu, J., R. Marodon, X. Ru, X. Ren, and X. Wu. 2021. "What Are Public Development Banks and Development Financing Institutions? Qualification Criteria, Stylized Facts and Development Trends." *China Economic Quarterly International* 1 (4): 271–94.

# NDFI Case Studies

## FIDEICOMISOS INSTITUIDOS EN RELACIÓN CON LA AGRICULTURA (MEXICO)

This section discusses the Fideicomisos Instituidos en Relación con la Agricultura (FIRA) in Mexico, including an overview of the institution and its green strategy and governance, green financing sources and uses, climate and environmental (C&E) risk management, and climate-related disclosures and reporting.

### Institutional overview

FIRA is composed of four trust funds administered by Banxico, the central bank of Mexico. FIRA's main objective is to facilitate and promote greater financing of agricultural activities by financial institutions, including agribusiness and other related economic activities in rural areas. The institution's main bylaws do not mention sustainability or climate-related goals; however, its mission is "to promote, until it is well established, an inclusive, sustainable, and productive agri-food and rural sector."[1]

FIRA provides loans and credit guarantees to financial institutions (FIs) operating as second-tier institutions, as well as technical assistance to rural producers and agricultural financial intermediaries. Approximately 60 percent of the total agricultural credit in Mexico originated by commercial banks is supported by FIRA.

### Green strategy and governance

FIRA's Institutional Program 2020–24 considers the National Financing Program for Development and the United Nations Sustainable Development Goals (SDGs) to formulate its goals for the period. One goal is to "contribute to the development of a responsible and sustainable agricultural, forestry, and fishing sector."[2] To attain that goal, a sustainability strategy was designed with three basic pillars: to avoid environmental harm, to finance green projects, and to catalyze support for green financing (refer to figure B.1).

FIRA is not part of Mexico's formal process to track or make decisions regarding the Nationally Determined Contributions (NDCs) per the Paris Agreement, and it does not have a specific reduction target assigned. Nevertheless, FIRA's activities aim to support the national efforts to reduce greenhouse gases

**FIGURE B.1**

**FIRA's Institutional Program, 2020–24**

| Priority objectives | Sustainability strategy basic pillars |
|---|---|
| Financial inclusion | 1. Not to harm the environment<br>  • Reduce FIRA's environmental footprint<br>  • Environmental and social risks administration systems<br>  • Participation in sustainability initiatives |
| Productivity | 2. Contribute to the solution<br>  • Project financing |
| Sustainability of the agricultural sector | 3. Involve others<br>  • Green bond issuance |

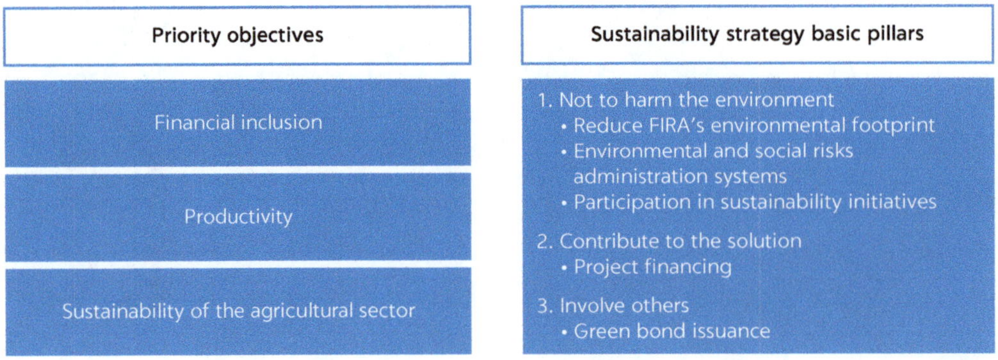

*Source:* FIRA's Institutional Program 2020-24, https://www.fira.gob.mx/Nd/Programa Institucional2020.pdf.
*Note:* FIRA = Fideicomisos Instituidos en Relación con la Agricultura.

(GHGs) and to adapt to the effects of climate change. Also, FIRA is actively involved in other sustainability-related financial initiatives, such as the United Nations Global Compact, the Sustainability Committee of the Mexican Bank Association, and the Consultative Council for Green Finance, all of which support the NDCs' goals through its activities.

In 2019, FIRA signed the Sustainability Protocol of the Mexican Bank Association, which requires that FIs' higher decision-making bodies are involved in C&E issues. A working group composed of the heads of the different FIRA departments involved in environmental issues periodically reports to the Technical Committee, the higher decision-making body at FIRA.

FIRA sets annual targets for its sustainability portfolio (that is, sustainable investment concepts [ICs]). For 2022, FIRA's sustainability target was 14,200 million pesos (approximately US$700 million). FIRA does not have a specialized exclusion list based on green targets. Nevertheless, in its credit decisions, FIRA relies on and considers the current national environmental and social (E&S) legislation.

FIRA plans to continue working with development partners to design sustainable financial products and programs financed in part with green bonds to improve its taxonomy and climate risk management systems and to obtain better climate information to use it more actively in its credit processes, as well as to make it available to the FIs and the producers accredited by those FIs. FIRA will continue to work to reduce the direct impacts of its activities on the environment, such as lower energy and water consumption in its offices and reduced paper consumption, among other activities.

## Green financing sources and uses

At the end of December 2021, FIRA's sustainability portfolio amounted to 14,247 million pesos (approx. US$700 million), 35 percent higher than the target annual amount for the year before. Its sustainable portfolio accounts for 5.9 percent of FIRA's loan portfolio and, by type of project, is as follows:

environmentally sustainable agriculture, 80.2 percent; efficient use of water, 6.4 percent; energy efficiency, 3.6 percent; and renewable energy, 9.8 percent.

FIRA has developed a few specialized sustainable financing programs with the support of several International Financial Organizations (IFOs). Examples include the following:

- The Pro-Sostenible Program, which provides an interest rate subsidy (cash back) to final borrowers of sustainable projects using donor funding;
- The Energy Efficiency Program, in which FIRA provides a technological guarantee, paying the difference between estimated and realized savings from the adoption of energy-efficient technologies using Green Technology Fund Resources; and
- The PROINFOR Program, through which FIRA supports FIs' loans to small forest producers and provides them with technical assistance so they can adopt sustainable production practices.

FIRA also has several credit guarantee schemes developed with other national entities such as the National Forest Fund and the Credit Guarantee Fund for the Efficient Use of Water. With those public resources, FIRA offers a higher guarantee for sustainable projects (65 percent versus the standard 40–50 percent guarantee) at no additional cost.

FIRA has identified several challenges to be addressed before scaling up green financing programs with IFOs:

- Lack of common definitions for green projects,
- Multiple objectives for sustainability projects that hamper implementation,
- Lack of homogeneous reporting standards on green benefits,
- Lack of legislation or guidelines on green financing to prevent greenwashing, and
- High supervision and verification costs of green projects.

FIRA funds itself from its own equity resources, IFOs' loans, and issues of securities in the domestic markets. The institution does not receive budgetary subsidies or funding from the central bank to provide subsidized lending.

FIRA has issued three green bonds (2019, 2020, and 2021) amounting to 8,000 million pesos (US$390 million) supporting more than 1,300 agricultural projects. Green bonds have been in great demand, but the interest rate has been about the same as that for more traditional bonds. FIRA has not yet issued sustainability-linked bonds and is not directly accredited by any international climate fund. However, the bank has accessed some of the international climate funds through other IFOs, such as the Inter-American Development Bank (IADB), Agence Française de Développement (AFD), or Kreditanstalt für Wiederaufbau (KFW).

## C&E risk management

FIRA does not expect that climate considerations will change its business model, but it recognizes the impact of climate change on agricultural production and the contribution of agriculture to climate change. FIRA's credit risk models do not include climate change considerations, mainly because of a lack of statistical information. Currently, no targets, tools, or metrics have been specified to assess C&E financial risks embedded in the risk management framework, and no regular climate stress testing is conducted.

Nevertheless, FIRA participated in a Drought Stress-Testing Tool study in 2017 to determine how incorporating drought scenarios by FIs has changed risk perception for their loan portfolios. FIRA also is currently participating in a study to identify the physical risks in the credit portfolio of FIs in Latin America using climate models and climate scenarios of the Intergovernmental Panel on Climate Change reports. Preliminary results identify water scarcity, more frequent droughts, lower agricultural productivity for main crops, and more extreme and intense climate events as the main risks. These exercises would help inform the strategy to manage climate-related financial risks.

FIRA's main challenges in identifying, assessing, monitoring, managing, and disclosing C&E financial risk include the following:

- Lack of access to information about potential quantitative effects of climate change,
- A portfolio of many small projects,
- Lack of the proper competencies to assess environmental and climate risks of the financial projects, and
- Difficulty communicating to the financial intermediaries with whom they operate and to the small producers and agribusinesses the importance of climate risks.

FIRA has developed, with the support of the IADB, an E&S risk analysis system (Sistema de Administracion de Riesgos Ambientales y Sociales [SARAS]) to factor social and environmental analysis and information into its credit decisions. SARAS is based on the Equator Principles and the Environmental, Health and Safety Guidelines of the International Financial Corporation (IFC). SARAS's analysis is applied to all loans above US$10 million funded with FIRA's resources (in line with the Equator Principles guidelines). An exclusion list for smaller loans is under consideration. SARAS analysis is based on information collected from producers.

FIRA does not analyze how institutions to which they lend administer environmental, social, and governance (ESG) risks, as the bank believes that the lack of regulation on the topic does not give it a strong rationale to do so. FIRA has never rejected a loan for climate reasons, but it has formulated conditions to address those concerns. However, in some cases, intermediaries have decided to fund those projects with their own sources.

## Climate-related disclosures and reporting

FIRA has developed a taxonomy to track green financing volumes with the support of the AFD and also has benefited from European Union resources from the Latin American Investment Facility. The taxonomy identifies 55 ICs that mitigate the adverse effects of agricultural activities on the environment. The FIs' loans supported by FIRA's resources on those 55 ICs constitute its sustainable portfolio, which is classified into four areas: environmentally sustainable agriculture, water efficiency, energy efficiency, and renewable energy. Among those, 29 ICs contribute to achieve lower GHG emissions and are part of its mitigation-financing portfolio. The taxonomy is based on AFD's sustainable dimensions.

With AFD support, FIRA is developing a methodology to identify what could be considered climate adaptation financing. The study has identified 88 ICs with positive contributions toward achieving a higher climate change adaptation of agricultural activities. The study also examined whether projects were located in municipalities considered by the Mexican environmental authorities (the National Institute of Ecology and Climate Change) to be vulnerable to climate change. Based on this study's preliminary results, FIRA's yearly total volume of climate adaptation finance is estimated at approximately 7,000 million pesos (approximately US$350 million). FIRA, as a second-tier institution operating through FIs by using loans and credit guarantees, tracks the level of private financing crowded in by its activities, including green activities.

FIRA does not report on C&E risk in line with the Task Force on Climate-Related Financial Disclosures (TCFD) recommendations. Nevertheless, FIRA reports all sustainability-related information in the "Memorias de Sostenibilidad," a yearly report published by FIRA that follows the Global Standards for Sustainability Reporting. FIRA's website has an ESG section. In addition, FIRA has started reporting using the standards of the Sustainability Accounting Standards Board, which identify the minimal set of financially material sustainability topics.

## KOREA DEVELOPMENT BANK (THE REPUBLIC OF KOREA)

This section discusses the Korea Development Bank (KDB) in the Republic of Korea, including an overview of the institution and its green strategy and governance, green financing sources and uses, C&E risk management, and climate-related disclosures and reporting.

### Institutional overview

The KDB, which has a core mandate to support Korea's sustainable growth, is a fully state-owned bank founded in 1954 to support Korea's development and policy agendas. Key priorities include deepening support for small and medium enterprises and enabling balanced economic development across regions. Although climate change and environmental protection are not explicit mandates, both are implicitly covered in KDB's broader mandate to support the country's sustainable growth.

### Green strategy and governance

KDB has published several commitments to the green agenda, including pledges to engage with the private sector to support climate investments and build technical expertise on key topics such as GHG accounting, climate risk assessments, and carbon markets. Beyond these broad commitments, KDB has developed an internal green financing strategy with the goal to support the government's NDC and 2050 carbon neutrality target. A key objective of this strategy is to increase the share of green financing to 16.8 percent of KDB's total annual financing by 2030.

In addition, KDB has established guidelines for coal financing and has published this information on its website. These guidelines prohibit the institution from supporting the construction and operation of new coal-fired power plants (KDB 2019).

KDB also actively participates in international initiatives to demonstrate its commitment to the green and sustainability agenda. For example, as a founding member of the International Development Finance Club (IDFC), KDB actively engages with other financial institutions on key topics related to climate financing. It also signed the United Nations Global Compact in 2007.

KDB is currently defining its internal governance framework to manage C&E issues. The Korea Development Bank Act states that KDB's business operations include providing funds for the development of the financial industry and national economy, such as fostering new growth engine industries and facilitating sustainable growth. KDB does not have a separate ESG-related organization within its board of directors, but the ESG Planning Department acts as a control tower for promoting green financing. KDB also has a Sustainability Committee that enables a bank-wide collaboration and produces detailed action plans for promoting ESG values and green financing.

## Green financing sources and uses

KDB leverages the labeled bond market as well as domestic and international public funding to support green investments. Since 2017, KDB has issued 15 green bonds and 11 social bonds in the domestic and international market through March 2022, raising an equivalent of US$6.7 billion, whereas during 2021, it funded an equivalent of US$2.8 billion through issuing green or social bonds, representing 5.1 percent of KDB's total funding that year. In the international market, KDB issued its first green bond under the 2017 Green Bond Framework, while the other 9 green bonds were issued under the 2019 Sustainable Bond Framework (KDB 2022). The proceeds from the green bonds were primarily leveraged to support renewable energy and clean transport projects, and KDB reported that these bonds would support the generation of 3,368 GWh of clean energy and 177,744 electric vehicles annually.

Not only did the issuance of green bonds mobilize the required financing for green investments, it also has supported the development of the country's green financing markets by raising the profile and demonstrating the feasibility of green bonds with potential issuers. In the domestic market, ₩3.7 trillion (equivalent to US$3 billion) of green bonds have been issued up to March 2022.

Beyond the labeled bond market, KDB has access to a national climate fund established by the government as part of supporting the country's NDC and 2050 carbon neutrality target, as well as the Green Climate Fund (GCF), accredited since 2016. For example, the Climate Action Fund, newly launched in 2021, has provided ₩130 billion in the same year for KDB's new green financing program (KDB Net-Zero Program). For the GCF, an accredited entity initially approved in December 2016 and reaccredited in May 2022, KDB has access to the GCF funds in pursuit of increasing climate actions in developing and emerging markets. GCF has recommended that KDB deploy the GCF funds in markets other than Korea, as the country is considered socioeconomically advanced.

KDB targets green investments in sectors that have a high funding gap but are key to achieving Korea's carbon neutrality goal. Beyond the green taxonomy, the government has developed a set of predefined criteria to identify green investments that should be prioritized for a Green New Deal. These criteria are now being used by 4 ministries and 11 public FIs, including KDB, to identify priority green investments, covering 77 items also related to the green taxonomy. To avoid crowding out the private sector, investments have targeted projects that are not commercially viable (for example, early-stage investments in nascent technology solutions such as carbon capture and storage and green hydrogen).

KDB supports private sector climate action by offering credit enhancements for green projects, conducting demonstration investments, and increasing the private sector's readiness to participate in climate policies. To crowd in private capital, KDB utilizes funding from the national climate fund to cover first losses of private sector green investments. KDB also lowers interest rates for certain green projects to increase the attractiveness of these investments. In addition, KDB conducts demonstration investments for green projects to build a track record and increase the private sector's confidence in investment areas with which they are less familiar.

Furthermore, KDB bolsters the private sector's participation in the labeled bond market by arranging, underwriting, and investing in green and sustainable bonds. In 2021, for the first time in Korea, KDB issued three primary collateralized bond obligations (P–CBOs) backed by privately placed ESG bonds issued by micro, small, and medium enterprises (MSMEs). These P–CBO transactions backed corporate capital investments in green projects and marked a milestone in an ESG bond market dominated by public offerings from large and public companies, extending the reach to MSMEs and private placements.

Finally, KDB plays a key role in facilitating the private sector's participation in the government's climate policy instruments. For example, KDB and five other banks are responsible for piloting the application of the Korean Green Taxonomy. KDB has also acted as a market maker for a national emissions-trading plan, with the goal of stimulating market liquidity by simultaneously selling and buying in the market (International Carbon Action Partnership ICAP 2019]).

## C&E risk management

In January 2017, KDB signed the Equator Principles and established environmental and social risk management (ESRM) policies and guidelines for project transactions in line with these principles. KDB's ESRM process follows several key steps:

1. *Identification,* to identify relevant projects;

2. *Categorization,* to categorize projects as low, medium, or high risk;

3. *Review,* to assess compliance with EP requirements;

4. *Financing documentation,* to incorporate covenants on the client's E&S undertaking into financial documents; and

5. *Monitoring and reporting,* to validate continued compliance.

KDB has taken initial steps to further integrate climate change into its risk management framework. ESRM is usually distinct from policies and procedures to manage climate risks because climate risk management requires forward-looking assessments, such as scenario analysis or stress testing, to estimate the future impact of these risks on investment and credit portfolios. KDB has not yet fully mainstreamed climate risk management practices in line with the Basel Committee on Banking Supervision (BCBS) Principles on climate risks (BCBS 2022).

Nonetheless, since 2021, KDB has been working to develop a climate risk analysis in line with the BCBS recommendations. As a starting point, KDB has conducted an assessment to evaluate KDB's exposure to climate transition risks.

An assessment of physical risks has not yet been conducted because KDB is waiting for supervisory guidance on the topic. Beyond risk assessments, KDB has also developed an innovative approach to integrate a capital buffer for transition risks.[3]

Moving forward, several challenges could limit KDB's ability to manage climate risks:

- Data limitations and
- Lack of supervisory guidance on climate scenario analysis and risk management.

## Climate-related disclosure and reporting

KDB is developing an internal framework for tracking and reporting on green financing. In addition to publishing its green and sustainable bond frameworks and related impact reports from the first quarter of every year on its website,[4] KDB is developing a framework for tracking green financing amounts based on the National Green Taxonomy. By piloting this taxonomy, KDB has identified 69 economic activities that can be considered green in line with the country's carbon neutrality target and other environmental goals (such as water conservation, biodiversity, and pollution prevention). This work forms the basis for tracking green financing and assessing progress toward KDB's target, which is to dedicate 16.8 percent of its financing to green investments.

KDB has regular disclosures of E&S risks, but disclosure of climate risks is limited. KDB has published annual reports on its implementation of the Equator Principles since 2018. The reports include information on its ESRM process and projects' exposure to E&S risks. While detailed disclosure and reporting on climate risks remains limited, KDB intends to adopt the TCFD framework by 2024.

## TÜRKIYE SINAI KALKINMA BANKASI (TÜRKIYE)

This section discusses the Türkiye Sinai Kalkinma Bankasi (TSKB) in Türkiye, including an overview of the institution and its green strategy and governance, green financing sources and uses, C&E risk management, and climate-related disclosures and reporting.

## Institutional overview

TSKB, Türkiye's privately owned development and investment bank, was established in 1950 with the support of the World Bank and the Central Bank of Türkiye. TSKB supports Türkiye's sustainable growth with corporate banking, investment banking, and advisory services provided to customers as a first- and second-tier lender. In the environmental and renewable-energy sectors, the bank ranks as number one in the number of projects financed in Türkiye. It is also the leading bank in Türkiye in promoting new initiatives for scaling up green financing, as well as in establishing governance arrangements and developing methodologies for C&E risks. In addition, TSKB raises awareness on climate change via the Green Swan Platform, where it has published "Climate Review" reports for the past 2 years.[5]

## Green strategy and governance

TSKB's mission is focused on sustainable development objectives and creating value for the inclusive and sustainable development of Türkiye through financing and advisory solutions (TSKB 2022a). TSKB started its sustainability journey in the 1980s with integrating environmental factors into loan evaluation processes. In the 1990s, the bank offered its first loan for environmental projects to the market, and in the 2000s, it began project financing in renewable energy (TSKB 2022d). As the concept of *sustainability* was gaining importance on a global scale, TSKB established the Environmental Management System in 2005 and the Sustainability Management System in 2012 to shape all business processes with a sustainability approach, including evaluating and managing E&S risks from lending activities and the institution's operational services (including maintaining its carbon-neutral banking activities), financing environmental projects, informing all stakeholders about sustainability issues, and disclosing to the public information regarding the E&S impact management processes and value created via the financing activities (TSKB 2022c).

TSKB's mission is operationalized within the Sustainability Policy adopted in 2012 and updated in 2022. This policy considers the E&S impacts of TSKB's activities, including the effects of climate change on economic and social welfare and growth (TSKB 2022e). In 2021, TSKB enacted the Climate Change Mitigation and Adaptation Policy to complement the Sustainability Policy to publicly communicate the basic principles of climate change. Among other actions, TSKB is committed to considering mitigation and adaptation to climate change in all its credit activities and internal operations (TSKB 2022b). This mitigation and adaptation is addressed in three main pillars within the scope of its Sustainability Strategy:

1. Supporting Türkiye's sustainable development model,

2. Playing an active role in tackling climate change, and

3. Contributing to Türkiye's industrial transition to a low-carbon economy.

C&E considerations are integrated in TSKB's governance arrangements. TSKB's organizational structure for sustainability involves the board of directors and the Executive Committee and comprises all employees. The board of directors guides the bank's operations in line with its sustainability strategy. All sustainability work, including coordination of activities and business plans, is conducted by two main pillars:

1. The Sustainability Committee, established in 2014 and consisting of four members of the board of directors as well as the chief executive officer and three executive vice presidents, and

2. The Sustainability Management Committee, chaired by the chief executive officer and led by three executive vice presidents with the heads of working groups from the departments responsible for rolling out sustainability activities throughout the bank.

Eleven working groups are under the Management Committee, each addressing different sustainability areas, including the Climate Risks Working Group established in 2020, which consists of three subgroups that work on physical risk, transition risk, and scenario analysis.

TSKB sets targets for greening its activities. Rather than using green financing terms, as there is no common green taxonomy in Türkiye yet, there are parameters such as ratio of SDG-linked loans and ratio of loans contributing to C&E SDGs. As announced in one of its Climate Risk Reports (TSKB 2021b), TSKB aims to have a 90-percent share of SDG-linked loans and a 60-percent share of C&E SDG-linked loans in the total portfolio by 2025.

In addition, TSKB intends to limit the share of power plants generating electricity from nonrenewable sources to 5 percent. Within the scope of its Climate Change Mitigation and Adaptation Policy, TSKB has declared it will not finance greenfield coal-fired thermal power plants and coal-mining investments for electricity generation. For its direct impact, TSKB aims to reduce its Scope 1 emissions by 42 percent by 2030 and by 63 percent by 2035. The bank also commits to continue sourcing 100 percent renewable electricity through 2035 and to have zero Scope 2 emissions. For Scope 3 emissions, in early 2022 TSKB's emissions associated with lending activities were calculated, verified, and published transparently for the first time in the Turkish financial sector. TSKB has submitted the science-based targets to the Science-Based Targets initiative for validation and is running the procedures for the United Nations (UN) Net-Zero Banking Alliance.

TSKB is committed to aligning its activities with international and national C&E goals. TSKB plays an active role in national and international initiatives in the field of sustainability (for example, United Nations Environment Programme [UNEP] FI, United Nations Global Compact, Global Reporting Initiative, and IDFC). In 2019, TSKB joined the UNEP FI Principles for Responsible Banking as a founding signatory as part of its sustainable banking activities.[6]

In its activities, TSKB considers the objectives and recommendations of the Paris Agreement, NDCs, and TCFD, among others. For example, the Climate Change Mitigation and Adaptation Policy announces the setup of targets and implementation of necessary actions to achieve GHG emissions in line with the long-term goals of the Paris Agreement. TSKB has set 1.5°C-aligned GHG reduction targets for Scope 1 emissions for 2030 and 2035, which contribute to the Paris Agreement's goals.

Furthermore, TSKB adopted the SDGs of the United Nations in 2015, reporting on its direct or indirect contribution to all 17 SDGs. TSKB also supports climate change–related activities and efforts at high-level global meetings, such as in the UN Conference of the Parties (2021).

At the national level, TSKB actively participates in forums on sustainability issues. For example, it is involved in the preparation of the Green Deal Action Plan of Türkiye by the Ministry of Commerce and other working groups (for example, Clean Energy, Zero Waste, Sustainable Production, and Consumption) in their related ministries; in the Sustainability Working Group within the Banking Regulation and Supervision Authority; with the Sustainability Committee within the Banks Association of Türkiye; and in workshops on the Climate Adaptation Action Plan by the Ministry of Environment, Urbanization and Climate Change. TSKB, along with its sustainability advisory company Escarus, was also an active member of two subcommittees of the Climate Council—GHG Reduction and Green Finance and Carbon Pricing—which was held in February 2022 in Konya. TSKB and Escarus representatives prepared draft recommendations of the committees with the cooperation of other participants.

TSKB has identified several challenges to scaling up its green financing:

- The regulatory environment is still under development, and no standardization exists for disclosures, taxonomy, data collection, and so forth.
- FIs often face insufficient financial resources. Even though the demand for resource-efficient investment and renewable-energy projects is high and can be further increased by properly raising consumer awareness, access to the long-term funding essential for project and investment finance can be limited.
- The macroeconomic environment is not always conducive for long-term investment. Fighting climate change, supporting the transition to a carbon-free economy, and ensuring inclusive social development will continue to be among TSKB's strategic priorities in the upcoming years. In this context, TSKB will continue to cooperate with Development Financial Institutions (DFIs) to provide long-term thematic funding and to shift its learning curve, as well as to increase its capacity via technical assistance programs.

## Green financing sources and uses

Currently, TSKB does not publicly disclose volumes of green assets; it also does not track climate adaptation financing. Via lending activities, the bank mainly supports seven SDGs, including combating and adapting to climate change. The share of SDG-linked loans has reached 93 percent of total loans. Loans linked to C&E SDGs account for 61 percent of loans, and these have contributed to a reduction of 12.2 million tons of $CO_2$ emissions per year (TSKB 2021b). In its loan portfolio, power generation has the largest share, at 39.7 percent, with renewable energy—mostly wind, geothermal, solar, and biogas or biomass resources—accounting for 89 percent of the power generation portfolio.

TSKB offers several financial products for green financing: conventional loans (working-capital loans, longer-term loans), project finance loans, and second-tier (or APEX) loans or thematic on-lending to other FIs. In addition, the bank provides technical assistance and consultancy services to its clients via Escarus (TSKB Sustainability Consultancy), for example, on thematic bond issuances. As of the end of 2021, the share of investment loans within the total loan portfolio narrowed to 62 percent, while the share of working-capital and APEX loans reached 32 percent and 6 percent, respectively. The increase in working-capital loans was associated with addressing the liquidity needs of MSMEs adversely affected by the COVID-19 pandemic.

In addition, TSKB recently introduced an SDG-linked lease certificate in line with its green transformation efforts in capital markets. TSKB plans to further develop various thematic credit lines (projects) with themes related to the circular economy, the promotion of green deals, climate change adaptation, and the creation of employment via green growth.

TSKB utilizes domestic and international funding sources, with ESG-linked funding reaching 80 percent in total liabilities. Although TSKB does not accept deposits, it does borrow from domestic and international money and loan markets, international capital markets, and international FIs and DFIs. Eighty-nine percent of the liabilities consist of foreign-exchange liabilities, with the majority of these being medium- and long-term funds obtained from abroad in foreign currency, including under the guarantee of the Ministry of Treasury and Finance. DFI funding is instrumental for extending long-term, reliable financing to eligible projects. In 2021, 100 percent of international borrowing was ESG-focused. In addition, TSKB is listed at Borsa Istanbul with a market value reaching US$308 million in 2021.

Funding through DFI accounts for 67 percent of TSKB's funding structure. TSKB works closely with the World Bank, IFC, the European Investment Bank (EIB), the Asian Infrastructure Investment Bank, AFD, KFW, the Japan Bank for International Cooperation, the China Development Bank, the European Bank for Reconstruction and Development, and others.

TSKB has demonstrated leadership in issuing green or sustainable bonds since 2016. TSKB had three green or sustainable bond issuances, for a total of US$1.05 billion. The first bond issuance was in 2016, followed by a sustainable subordinated bond issuance in 2017 and a sustainable bond issuance in 2021. Funds obtained through bonds are used to finance green and social projects in line with the Sustainable Finance Framework. TSKB submits an Impact Report to its investors annually to provide them with insight into the effects of the projects financed through the funds from the bond issuances. In addition, apart from sustainable bilateral borrowing agreements, TSKB funding includes syndicated loans tied to an ESG rating and sustainability performance criteria. In 2021, the syndicated loans were linked to sustainability criteria, namely the gender pay gap, an exit from coal financing, and COVID-19 financing themes.

## C&E risk management

TSKB expects that C&E risks will affect its business model and defines climate risks and opportunities from the internationally recognized perspective of physical and transition risks. TSKB examines *direct* (focuses on the effects of climate change from TSKB's operations and activities) and *indirect* (focuses on the effects of climate change from TSKB's products and services, as well as its loan portfolio) risks and opportunities, having metrics and targets for both. For example, TSKB monitors its Scope 1, 2, and 3 emissions and measures its electricity, natural gas, water, and paper consumption, as well as the amount of its glass, plastic, and paper waste. TSKB has calculated Scope 3 emissions of companies that are financed by the bank and operate in carbon-intensive industries (for example, nonrenewable power generation, cement, iron, and steel).[7] These loans accounted for 7.5 percent of TSKB's 2021 year-end portfolio, where the emissions calculated accounted for nearly 70 percent of the whole loan book. For indirect impact, TSKB monitors the following key performance indicators: the number of renewable energy projects funded, the total installed capacity of renewable-energy projects funded, its share in Türkiye's renewable energy, the contribution to the reduction of $CO_2$ emissions, the share of electricity generation in the loan portfolio, the share of renewable and nonrenewable energy in the electricity generation portfolio, and the share of sustainability-themed loans.

Climate-related risks and opportunities are identified in the short, medium, and long term; their effects on the organization's activities, strategy, and financial structure are analyzed, and actionable plans are prepared. Since 2005, TSKB has been quantifying the E&S risks inherent in every project as well as from its own operations. TSKB identifies impacts and manages risks from its own operations via the International Organization for Standardization (ISO) 14001 Environmental Management System certification. The bank aims to reduce emissions every year and has been offsetting its carbon footprint for remaining emissions since 2009 through buying Gold Standard carbon certificates.

TSKB evaluates and manages E&S impacts from its lending operations using its Environmental and Social Risk Evaluation Tool (ERET), applied to all projects since 2007. ERET rates projects on 5 criteria under 35 headings.[8] The bank also considers the GHG emissions and energy and resource efficiency dimensions of its financed projects. The results of such evaluations are considered in the project assessment, financing, and investment-monitoring processes. Customers then take measures to prevent or mitigate negative E&S impacts as well as draft Environmental and social management Plans. TSKB's Engineering Team, which also includes a social specialist, regularly monitors the performance of clients in managing the E&S impacts, in line with the E&S Action Plans.

TSKB's assessment of physical and transition risks arising from climate change and their integration into all loan processes are ongoing. In addition to ERET, in 2022, TSKB developed an in-house assessment tool for measuring the physical and transition risks in financed projects and companies and introduced mitigation plans for these risks in the loan allocation process. The work allows TSKB to be aware of these risks at an early stage to mitigate the climate-related credit risk and negative substantive financial impacts. This tool is currently integrated into TSKB's credit evaluation criteria, and the evaluation results are submitted to the Credit Committee. TSKB plans to integrate climate change–related risks into its loan evaluation, allocation, and monitoring processes by the end of 2023.

The bank evaluates the impact of climate change on its portfolio, with scenario analysis and stress testing currently under development. Climate-related risks are identified through a sector-based heat map that will be used as a basis for scenario analysis and stress testing. In 2020, 69 percent of the cash loan portfolio was identified as being at high or medium risk in terms of physical risk and 38 percent in terms of transition risk.[9] In addition, TSKB uses case studies for sectors that are prevalent in its portfolio and are vulnerable to climate change (for example, hydroelectric power plants for physical risk, the cement industry for transition risk).

Scenario analysis and stress testing are still works in progress, and methodologies are to be further developed, with a more detailed assessment of asset resilience against climate risks planned. Scenario analysis and stress-testing tools will be used to identify the potential consequences of climate-related risks and opportunities under different time constraints and conditions, with the results included in business processes and strategic planning. The Scenario Analysis Subworking Group uses different scenario analyses prepared by respectable institutions (such as the International Energy Agency, Intergovernmental Panel on Climate Change, and World Resources Institute) to further evaluate and integrate the results into their climate risk scenario analysis. In addition, TSKB focuses on the targets Türkiye develops in its climate policies. The main difficulties faced are data availability and the current use of methodologies that do not allow historical data to inform the future, therefore weakening the predictability of climate risks.

## Climate-related disclosure and reporting

TSKB monitors and classifies its portfolio using taxonomy based on sector and theme. Although a national taxonomy is planned to be developed by the end of 2023, TSKB uses its own taxonomy, with 11 sectors identified for loan tagging: renewable electricity generation; nonrenewable electricity generation; electricity power distribution; natural gas distribution; agriculture and livestock; the manufacturing industry; the service sector; finance; construction and contracting; retail; and telecommunications, information technology, and media.[10] Some sectors are also divided into subsectors.

TSKB monitors its green portfolio and provides disclosures in line with TCFD. TSKB's sustainability reporting practice started in 2009 and has evolved into integrated reporting in 2016. Since 2018, TSKB has illustrated its strategy, targets, performance, value creation plan, and impacts driven by its operations via its Integrated Annual Reports, which are verified by an auditor. The bank publicly discloses information on climate-related risks. In 2021, and for the first time in the Turkish financial sector, TSKB issued its first climate risk report prepared in line with TCFD recommendations. The bank also discloses its practices and initiatives annually via the Carbon Disclosure Project reports.

## DEVELOPMENT BANK OF SOUTHERN AFRICA (SOUTH AFRICA)

This section discusses the Development Bank of Southern Africa (DBSA) in South Africa, including an overview of the institution and its green strategy and governance, green financing sources and uses, C&E risk management, and climate-related disclosures and reporting.

### Institutional overview

DBSA, a leading DFI in Africa, was established in 1983 and is wholly owned by the government of South Africa. DBSA's mandate is to promote economic growth and regional integration for sustainable development projects in South Africa, the Southern African Development Community, and Sub-Saharan Africa. The bank does this work by mobilizing funding for projects that build sustainable infrastructure across the continent.

DBSA is mandated to invest predominantly in South Africa, with 40 percent of its investment book geared toward infrastructure in the rest of Africa. The client base includes municipalities, the private sector, state-owned enterprises, sovereigns, and public-private partnerships.

### Green governance and strategy

Several frameworks and strategies are guiding DBSA's activities in green financing. In 2021, DBSA approved the Just Transition Investment Framework to guide the bank's approach to support the drive to becoming greener. This framework will support institutional activities for a Just Transition in alignment with the Paris Agreement as part of its pathway to becoming net-zero by 2050. The framework also informs DBSA's Integrated Sustainable Development Approach (ISDA). The objective of developing an integrated approach is to mainstream green initiatives across the bank to ensure that it meets global good practice standards across all sectors and financing activities, including using a mandatory assessment throughout the investment approval process and utilizing enhanced appraisal methodologies and tools, such as E&S safeguards.

With its "Statement on Net-Zero," DBSA publicly announced in 2021 its commitment to playing an active role in a Just Transition that achieves net-zero emissions by 2050. This statement is an important signal to showcase DBSA's aim to support the financing of the implementation of global, regional, and national initiatives related to the low-carbon transition.[11] For example, this work includes alignment with South Africa's NDC through the implementation of dedicated climate programs.[12]

Several governance arrangements and committees are in place to support DBSA's C&E objectives. Through its governance structures, including the board of directors (and its subcommittees), Investment Committee, and the Infrastructure Delivery and Knowledge Committee, DBSA ensures that C&E factors are considered in investment decisions. A clear commitment has been made from the top, a key factor to support DBSA in delivering on its climate and green financing commitments. Overall, the number of full-time staff directly responsible for implementing DBSA's green and climate-financing activities, as well as C&E risk management, has been enhanced.

To further support the agenda, DBSA has established a dedicated Climate and Environmental Finance Unit that provides dedicated advisory, investment, and implementation support to access funds from climate-financing mechanisms such as the Global Environment Facility (GEF), GCF, and so forth. The accreditation with GEF and GCF allows DBSA to leverage its funds to support its C&E objectives. Partnership with the various C&E–financing mechanisms further helps the bank benchmark and improve, among other aspects, its fiduciary duty and environmental and social standards (ESS). frameworks against international standards. The ESG Unit is responsible for undertaking E&S due diligence, monitoring, policy, and framework development as well as supporting the development and implementation of the bank's ISDA.

Other related technical committees include the Just Transition Strategy Committee and the Social and Ethics Committee, which ensure adequate reporting on environmental indicators and effective application of DBSA's ESS. Moreover, several internal climate and ESG-related-training and capacity-building programs are upskilling DBSA staff to enhance effective ISDA implementation.

## Green financing sources and uses

In 2018, DBSA set a target of at least 30 percent of all its investments contributing to climate goals. This percentage is subdivided into a 70-percent target for mitigation and a 30-percent target for adaptation. DBSA is currently reviewing the targets in the Just Transition Investment Framework's development and expects that new and more ambitious targets will be set as part of the review process. The development of climate-financing targets enables DBSA to define its commitments toward national and international climate change policies and communicate its intentions to its shareholders and stakeholders. Moreover, all DBSA climate programs are designed to crowd in private investment for low-carbon energy and clean water infrastructure, using limited public funds. For example, the Climate Finance Facility (CFF) target is to reach an overall portfolio private finance leverage ratio of 1:5.

DBSA has been tracking its green financing volumes for the past 5 years and recently has completed a green deep dive to obtain a more detailed understanding of its loan book. The green deep dive used the IDFC taxonomy to determine the portion of the DBSA portfolio that is carbon-intensive, green, or uncategorized. This study will be used to plan the Just Transition Strategy and targets, as well as to monitor the bank's portfolio composition.

Most of DBSA's green loans are for climate mitigation projects, mainly in renewable energy. DBSA is also actively financing energy-efficiency projects to support emissions reductions throughout Southern Africa. A small portion of the green loans is directed toward financing climate adaptation projects, pointing to the challenges in finding bankable adaptation projects. Other green projects are related to water, waste, biodiversity, and agriculture.

DBSA can draw on numerous sources of national and international funding for its C&E activities. National funding sources include commitments from South Africa's National Treasury and various national climate programs. At the international level, DBSA has received support and credit lines from different Multilateral Development Banks, including the World Bank and the EIB, as well as bilateral partners. DBSA was accredited by the GEF in 2021 and has been reaccredited by the GCF for a second term until October 2027.

To complement these financing sources, DBSA entered the green bond market in 2021. DBSA's first green bond was issued in 2021 through a private placement. This €200 million bond was supported by the AFD and is structured in alignment with DBSA's Green Bond Framework.[13] The proceeds of this first issuance were used mainly for financing and refinancing renewable-energy projects. This green bond was externally verified and contributed to proving the business case for renewables in the region. A second green bond was also launched in 2021, again issued through a private placement. The proceeds of the US$210 million issuance were used to refinance renewable-energy generation and transmission projects, in addition to adding to DBSA's pool of liquidity for future green power generation projects. DBSA is currently developing an integrated Sustainability Bond Framework, which aims to guide the issuance of both sustainability and sustainability-linked bonds in the future.

Different instruments are offered to support scaling up green financing, including credit enhancements and grants. Supported by the GCF, DBSA launched the CFF, a lending facility designed to increase climate-related investment in Southern Africa by addressing market barriers and focusing on blended finance mechanisms and credit enhancements, such as subordinated debt and tenor extensions. CFF is the first private sector climate-financing facility in Africa using a "green bank model," with the aim to de-risk and increase the bankability of climate projects to crowd in private sector investment. Also supported by the GCF, the Embedded Generation Investment Programme offers a credit support mechanism that enables funding of embedded-generation renewable-energy projects through the provision of risk capital for projects implemented by private sector entities and local municipalities.

Besides financial instruments, DBSA provides project preparation support to further facilitate the development of green bankable projects and climate programs. Through its accreditation with the GCF, DBSA can access project preparation funding to build a pipeline of projects. The GCF Project Preparation Facility Grant helps the bank undertake various project preparation activities—including feasibility studies, ESG studies, and advisory services—to support financial structuring. To date, DBSA has successfully used Project Preparation Facility Grant support from the GCF to design innovative climate programs, including energy efficiency, municipal solid waste, and water reuse programs.

DBSA cites several interlinking challenges inhibiting the scaling up of green financing:

- Reporting requirements for green projects can be onerous, requiring sufficient capacity to effectively monitor these projects and presenting a significant barrier if reporting and the level of capacity for similar nongreen projects is not needed.
- Pipeline development and the bankability of projects are key issues emphasizing the need for more support at the project preparation stage. Even where de-risking instruments are available, projects may not be bankable owing to a lack of capacity and expertise to develop bankable projects.
- Seeking accreditation and subsequently accessing concessional financing from the global climate finance mechanisms of the United Nations Framework Convention on Climate Change is a long, cumbersome process, with requirements that can be challenging to implement practically, leaving green financing opportunities untapped. Mobilizing finance for climate adaptation from these mechanisms is challenging, especially in the absence of readily available climate data. Furthermore, the lack of lending options using local currency with these mechanisms can result in risks due to exposure to high foreign exchange rates and costly hedging structures, further complicating program implementation.

## C&E risk management

DBSA has a strong E&S management system. Impact-related E&S risk assessments are a core component of DBSA's project appraisal, negotiation, disbursement, and monitoring processes. In 2021, DBSA formalized its environmental appraisal framework for project assessments. This framework entails a sound and detailed approach to assess environmental risks throughout the due diligence process, with work ongoing to also integrate biodiversity frameworks. The appraisal framework now also considers how climate-related risks can impact lending activities. High-risk projects are required to undergo a more detailed assessment and provide associated target and metrics monitoring.

Further work is planned to integrate the consideration of C&E financial risks into DBSA's activities. The institution demonstrates awareness of the potential impacts of climate-related risks on its business operations, identifying the physical and transition risks to which it could be exposed, as well as the potential associated reputational risks. Standardization and formalization of the consideration of C&E financial risks has been identified as one priority under the ISDA. To manage and mitigate climate risk more effectively, DBSA is working to integrate climate risk into the existing Environmental and Social Management System and Development Results Reporting Framework. The institution also is considering the incorporation of climate-related risks and vulnerabilities into the deal-pricing process.

To support the development of internal and external capacity and integrate climate- and nature-related risks, vulnerabilities, and opportunities into its systems, DBSA is engaging with its partner DFIs and external stakeholders. One key challenge is the availability of information on development results and baseline data required to monitor and mitigate C&E risks and vulnerabilities.

## Climate-related disclosure and reporting

Although DBSA is seeking alignment with TCFD recommendations, it has not yet issued its own climate-related disclosure. However, DBSA is reviewing its existing Climate Change Policy Framework and developing a new toolkit to promote TCFD and other global standards. The intention is to develop more standardized disclosure and reporting practices that are better aligned with TCFD and to support the integration of climate risk into DBSA's activities more broadly.

Green financing reporting and tracking are based on DBSA's Development Results Reporting Framework. This framework is aligned with international good practice and covers the TCFD, the Taskforce on Nature-Related Financial Disclosures, and the National Treasury's green financing taxonomy, as well as the reporting requirements of partners and funders. DBSA also has used the IDFC taxonomy to classify projects under sectors and subsectors. This classification includes climate adaptation, mitigation, and other environmental activities. The latter includes projects related to water, biodiversity, and integrated waste management that promote the green economy and sustainability but have no significant or direct climate adaptation or mitigation objectives or co-benefits. DBSA has developed the Development Results Reporting Framework, a flexible, responsive tool to enable the bank to effectively report on its development and impact results, including green financing, SDGs, climate, gender, and other sustainability reporting requirements.

## NOTES

1. See the mission statement on FIRA's website: https://www.fira.gob.mx/Nd/VisionMisionValores.jsp.
2. See FIRA's Institutional Program 2020-24: https://www.fira.gob.mx/Nd/ProgramaInstitucional2020.pdf.
3. KDB has set aside ₩0.7 trillion as a capital buffer for transition risks as part of its 2022 risk management framework. The capital buffer was established based on a transition risk stress test that estimated the probability of default under the Net-Zero 2050 scenario of the Network of Central Banks and Supervisors for Greening the Financial System framework.
4. The impact reports include detailed information on the functions and impact of the green bonds (for example, type of green projects supported, amount disbursed, and estimated tons of $CO_2$ reduced) (for example, refer to KDB 2022).
5. TSKB (Türkiye Sinai Kalkinma Bankasi) Research Reports. https://www.tskb.com.tr/en/research-reports/economic-research/climate-review.
6. TSKB initiated carbon-neutral banking practice in 2008 and became a signatory to the IDFC Climate Declaration in 2015, to the UNEP FI Principles for Responsible Banking in 2019, and to the Sustainable and Resilient Global Recovery and Biodiversity Declarations in 2020.
7. Refer to TSKB (2021b, 79).
8. The model rates electricity consumption, water consumption, and GHG emission levels to measure the impact of projects on climate change and their contribution to adaptation.
9. Refer to TSKB (2021a).
10. Refer to TSKB (2021a).
11. See DBSA's Statement on Net Zero: https://www.dbsa.org/press-releases/dbsa-statement-net-zero.
12. These programs include the Climate Finance Facility (CFF), Embedded Generation Investment Program, and Water Reuse Programs. The CFF focuses on specific climate investment opportunities based on a country's needs and sectoral priorities. The program aims to align and adapt its investment focus in accordance with the primary mitigation and adaption interventions outlined in the respective NDCs for each target country.

13. The Green Bond Framework received a Second Party Opinion Statement from Carbon Trust assessing its alignment with the Green Bond Principles (see evaluation report: https://www.dbsa.org/sites/default/files/media/documents/2021-03/Evaluation%20 of%20the%20DBSA%20Green%20Bond%20Framework%20and%20Green%20Bond .pdf).

## BIBLIOGRAPHY

BCBS (Basel Committee on Banking Supervision). 2022. *Principles for the Effective Management and Supervision of Climate-Related Financial Risks*. Basel, Switzerland: BCBS. https://www .bis.org/bcbs/publ/d532.pdf.

ICAP (International Carbon Action Partnership). 2019. *Korea Names "Market Makers" to Increase Liquidity*. Berlin, Germany: ICAP. https://icapcarbonaction.com/es/node/641.

KDB (Korea Development Bank). 2019. *Guidelines for Coal Financing*. https://www.kdb.co.kr /CHGLIR05N00.act?_mnuId=IHIHEN0028&JEX_LANG=EN.

KDB (Korea Development Bank). 2022. *Investor Newsletter*. https://www.kdb.co.kr /CHGLIR05N00.act?_mnuId=IHIHEN0028&JEX_LANG=EN.

TSKB (Türkiye Sinai Kalkinma Bankasi). 2021a. *Climate Risk Report on Task Force on Climate-Related Financial Disclosures*. https://www.tskb.com.tr/i/assets/document/pdf /TCFD-eng-2021-05-24.pdf.

TSKB (Türkiye Sinai Kalkinma Bankasi). 2021b. *Impact Oriented Sustainable Development: TSKB Integrated Annual Report 2021*. https://www.tskb.com.tr/uploads/file/tskb-2021 -integrated-report.pdf.

TSKB (Türkiye Sinai Kalkinma Bankasi). 2022a. "About Us." https://www.tskb.com.tr/en /about-us.

TSKB (Türkiye Sinai Kalkinma Bankasi). 2022b. *Climate Change Mitigation and Adaptation Policy*. https://www.tskb.com.tr/i/assets/document/pdf/TSKB%20Climate%20 Change%20Mitigation%20and%20Adaptation%20Policy.pdf.

TSKB (Türkiye Sinai Kalkinma Bankasi). 2022c. "Sustainability Management System." https:// www.tskb.com.tr/en/services/sustainable-banking/strategy-and-management /sustainability-management-system.

TSKB (Türkiye Sinai Kalkinma Bankasi). 2022d. "Sustainable Banking." https://www.tskb.com .tr/en/services/sustainable-banking.

TSKB (Türkiye Sinai Kalkinma Bankasi). 2022e. "Sustainability Policy." https://www.tskb.com .tr/en/services/sustainable-banking/our-policy/tskb-sustainability-policy.

www.ingramcontent.com/pod-product-compliance
Lightning Source LLC
Chambersburg PA
CBHW082108210326
41599CB00033B/6637